D1428075

GREAT
VEG

GREAT VEG

COLLINS & BROWN

The Good Housekeeping website is
www.goodhousekeeping.co.uk

ISBN 978-1-909397-04-0

A catalogue record for this book is available from
the British Library.

Reproduction by Dot Gradations Ltd, UK
Printed and bound by
1010 Printing International Ltd, China

This book can be ordered direct from the publisher.
Contact the marketing department, but try your
bookshop first.

www.anovabooks.com

NOTES

Both metric and imperial measures are given for
the recipes. Follow either set of measures, not a
mixture of both, as they are not interchangeable.

All spoon measures are level.
1 tsp = 5ml spoon; 1 tbsp = 15ml spoon.

Ovens and grills must be preheated to the specified
temperature.

Medium eggs should be used except where
otherwise specified. Free-range eggs are
recommended.

Note that some recipes contain raw or lightly
cooked eggs. The young, elderly, pregnant women
and anyone with an immune-deficiency disease
should avoid these because of the slight risk of
salmonella.

Contents

UCB
196195

Starters and Sides

A Vegetarian and Vegan Diet

Many people assume that a vegetarian's diet is automatically healthier than that of a carnivore. This isn't always the case – there are good and bad vegetarian diets. It is not enough simply to stop eating meat: the nutrients that would normally be obtained from meat must be replaced. As with any diet, variety is important. It is useful to have a basic understanding of nutrition and the importance of certain foods – if only to convince meat-eaters that a vegetarian diet can be healthy.

A vegetarian diet

A vegetarian diet is one that excludes meat, poultry and fish. Many vegetarians also avoid other animal products such as gelatine, animal fats such as lard and suet, and animal rennet in non-vegetarian cheeses. However, the majority of vegetarians do eat dairy produce, including milk, cheese and free-range eggs. It's quite common for vegetarians to rely too heavily on dairy products such as cheese and eggs, which can be high in saturated fats and calories. Such a limited diet is not only unhealthy but will also eventually become boring and tedious. As with any diet, variety is important.

Provided that a vegetarian diet includes a good range of cereals and grains, pulses, nuts and seeds, fruit and vegetables, dairy and/or soya products, it is unlikely to be nutritionally deficient, but, again, variety is important to ensure a good intake of protein.

A vegan diet

Vegans follow a more restrictive diet, which excludes, in addition to meat, poultry and fish, all dairy products, eggs, and even foods such as honey (because it is produced by bees). A vegan diet can be deficient in vitamin B12 (see page 37), which is only present in animal and dairy foods. To make up for this, fortified breakfast cereals, yeast extract and/or soya milk should be consumed. Soya products are a particularly valuable source of protein, energy, vitamin B12, vitamin D, calcium, minerals and beneficial omega-3 fatty acids.

Protein

Contrary to popular belief, there are lots of good vegetable sources of protein, such as beans, grains, nuts, soya products and Quorn, as well as eggs, cheese, milk and yogurt. Protein is made up of smaller units called amino acids. These are needed for the manufacture and repair of body cells, so they are very important. The body can manufacture some amino acids itself, but others, known as the essential amino acids, must come from food. Animal protein contains almost all of these and is therefore known as a 'complete' protein.

With the exception of soya products, vegetable proteins are lacking or low in one or more amino acids. However, by eating certain foods together at the same meal, any deficiency is overcome. This isn't as complicated as it sounds and usually happens automatically when menu planning. For example, pulses and nuts should be eaten with cereals or dairy products – such as muesli with yogurt or milk, chilli beans with rice, nut roast made with breadcrumbs, peanut butter on toast, dhal with raita, or nut burgers with a bap. (See also page 38.)

Beetroot Soup

Hands-on time: 15 minutes
Cooking time: about 45 minutes

1 tbsp olive oil

1 onion, finely chopped

750g (1lb 11oz) raw beetroot, peeled and cut into 1cm (½in) cubes

275g (10oz) potatoes, roughly chopped

2 litres (3½ pints) hot vegetable stock

juice of 1 lemon

8 tbsp soured cream

50g (2oz) mixed root vegetable crisps

salt and freshly ground black pepper

2 tbsp chopped chives to garnish

1 Heat the oil in a large pan, add the onion and cook for 5 minutes. Add the beetroot and potatoes and cook for a further 5 minutes.

2 Add the hot stock and lemon juice, then bring to the boil. Season with salt and ground black pepper, then reduce the heat and simmer, half-covered, for 25 minutes.

3 Leave the soup to cool a little, then whiz in batches in a blender or food processor until smooth. Pour the soup into a clean pan and reheat gently – do not boil.

4 Ladle into warmed bowls. Add 1 tbsp soured cream to each bowl, sprinkle with black pepper, top with a few vegetable crisps and sprinkle the chopped chives on top to serve.

FREEZE AHEAD

To make ahead and freeze, prepare the soup to the end of step 3, then cool, pack and freeze in a sealed container. It will keep for up to three months. To use, thaw the soup in the fridge overnight. Reheat gently and simmer over a low heat for 5 minutes. Complete step 4 to serve.

Serves 8

Courgette and Leek Soup

Hands-on time: 15 minutes
Cooking time: about 40 minutes

1 tbsp olive oil

1 onion, finely chopped

2 leeks, trimmed and sliced

900g (2lb) courgettes, grated

1.3 litres (2¼ pints) hot vegetable
  stock

4 short rosemary sprigs

1 small baguette

125g (4oz) grated Gruyère
  (see page 22)

salt and freshly ground black pepper

1 Heat the oil in a large pan. Add the onion and leeks and cook for 5–10 minutes. Add the courgettes and cook, stirring, for a further 5 minutes.

2 Add the hot stock and three of the rosemary sprigs, then bring to the boil. Season with salt and ground black pepper, then reduce the heat and simmer for 20 minutes.

3 Meanwhile, preheat the grill to medium-high. Slice the bread diagonally into eight and grill for 1–2 minutes on one side until golden. Turn the bread over, sprinkle with the cheese and season. Grill for a further 1–2 minutes. Keep the croûtes warm.

4 Leave the soup to cool a little. Remove the rosemary stalks and whiz the soup in batches in a blender or food processor until smooth. Pour into a clean pan and reheat gently – do not boil.

5 Ladle into warmed bowls, garnish with the croûtes, sprinkle with the remaining rosemary leaves and serve.

Serves 8

Keep it Seasonal

Why? Because the produce you buy will taste fantastic and cost less. Look out for good deals at supermarkets, farm shops, markets and greengrocers where you can sometimes buy larger, cheaper quantities for freezing or batch cooking. Pick Your Own farms often charge half the price of the supermarkets. You can pick fruit and vegetables at their ripest and enjoy a fun day out with the family too.

	Vegetables	Fruit
JANUARY	Beetroot, Brussels sprouts, cauliflower, celeriac, celery, chicory, Jerusalem artichoke, kale, leeks, parsnips, potatoes (maincrop), rhubarb, swede, turnips	Apples, clementines, kiwi fruit, lemons, oranges, passion fruit, pears, pineapples, pomegranates, satsumas, tangerines, walnuts
FEBRUARY	Brussels sprouts, cauliflower, celeriac, chicory, kale, leeks, parsnips, potatoes (maincrop), rhubarb, swede	Bananas, blood oranges, kiwi fruit, lemons, oranges, passion fruit, pears, pineapples, pomegranates
MARCH	Cauliflower, chicory, kale, leeks, purple sprouting broccoli, rhubarb, spring onions	Bananas, blood oranges, kiwi fruit, lemons, oranges, passion fruit, pineapples, pomegranates
APRIL	Asparagus, broccoli, Jersey royal potatoes, purple sprouting broccoli, radishes, rhubarb, rocket, spinach, spring onions, watercress	Bananas, kiwi fruit
MAY	Asparagus, broccoli, Jersey royal potatoes, new potatoes, radishes, rhubarb, rocket, spinach, spring onions, watercress	Cherries, kiwi fruit, strawberries
JUNE	Artichokes, asparagus, aubergines, broad beans, broccoli, carrots, courgettes, fennel, mangetouts, Jersey royal potatoes, new potatoes, peas, radishes, rocket, runner beans, spring onions, turnips, watercress	Cherries, strawberries

	Vegetables	Fruit
JULY	Artichokes, aubergines, beetroot, broad beans, broccoli, carrots, courgettes, cucumber, fennel, French beans, garlic, mangetouts, new potatoes, onions, peas, potatoes (maincrop), radishes, rocket, runner beans, turnips, watercress	Apricots, blackberries, blueberries, cherries, gooseberries, greengages, kiwi fruit, melons, peaches, raspberries, redcurrants, strawberries, tomatoes
AUGUST	Artichokes, aubergines, beetroot, broad beans, broccoli, carrots, courgettes, cucumber, fennel, French beans, garlic, leeks, mangetouts, marrow, new potatoes, onions, peas, peppers, potatoes (maincrop), radishes, rocket, runner beans, sweetcorn, watercress	Apricots, blackberries, blueberries, damsons, greengages, kiwi fruit, melons, nectarines, peaches, plums, raspberries, redcurrants, tomatoes
SEPTEMBER	Artichokes, aubergines, beetroot, broccoli, butternut squash, carrots, courgettes, cucumber, fennel, garlic, leeks, mangetouts, marrow, onions, parsnips, peas, peppers, potatoes (maincrop), radishes, rocket, runner beans, sweetcorn, watercress, wild mushrooms	Apples, blackberries, damsons, figs, grapes, melons, nectarines, peaches, pears, plums, raspberries, redcurrants, tomatoes, walnuts
OCTOBER	Artichokes, beetroot, broccoli, butternut squash, carrots, celeriac, celery, fennel, kale, leeks, marrow, onions, parsnips, potatoes (maincrop), pumpkin, swede, turnips, watercress, wild mushrooms	Apples, chestnuts, figs, pears, quince, tomatoes, walnuts
NOVEMBER	Artichokes, beetroot, Brussels sprouts, celeriac, celery, chicory, kale, leeks, parsnips, potatoes (maincrop), pumpkin, swede, turnips, watercress, wild mushrooms	Apples, chestnuts, clementines, cranberries, figs, passion fruit, pears, quince, satsumas, tangerines, walnuts
DECEMBER	Beetroot, Brussels sprouts, cauliflower, celeriac, celery, chicory, kale, leeks, parsnips, potatoes (maincrop), pumpkin, swede, turnips	Apples, chestnuts, clementines, cranberries, passion fruit, pears, pineapple, pomegranate, satsumas, tangerines, walnuts

Cheesy Polenta with Tomato Sauce

Hands-on time: 15 minutes
Cooking time: about 50 minutes, plus cooling

oil to grease and brush

225g (8oz) polenta

4 tbsp freshly chopped herbs, such as
   oregano, chives and flat-leafed parsley

100g (3½oz) freshly grated Parmesan
   (see page 22), plus fresh Parmesan
   shavings to serve

salt and freshly ground black pepper

For the tomato and basil sauce

1 tbsp vegetable oil

3 garlic cloves, crushed

500g carton creamed tomatoes
   or passata

1 bay leaf

1 fresh thyme sprig

caster sugar

3 tbsp freshly chopped basil, plus extra
   to garnish

1 Lightly oil a 25.5 × 18cm (10 × 7in)
   dish. Bring 1.1 litres (2 pints) water
   and ¼ tsp salt to the boil in a large
   pan. Sprinkle in the polenta, whisking
   constantly. Reduce the heat and
   simmer, stirring frequently, for 10–15
   minutes until the mixture leaves the
   sides of the pan.

2 Stir in the herbs and grated Parmesan
   and season to taste with salt and
   ground black pepper. Turn into the
   prepared dish and leave to cool.

3 Next, make the tomato and basil
   sauce. Heat the oil in a pan and fry the
   garlic for 30 seconds (do not brown).
   Add the creamed tomatoes or passata,
   the bay leaf, thyme and a large pinch
   of sugar. Season with salt and ground
   black pepper and bring to the boil,
   then reduce the heat and simmer,
   uncovered, for 5–10 minutes. Remove
   the bay leaf and thyme sprig and add
   the chopped basil.

4 To serve, cut the polenta into pieces and lightly brush with oil. Preheat a griddle and fry for 3–4 minutes on each side, or grill under a preheated grill for 7–8 minutes on each side. Serve with the tomato and basil sauce, fresh Parmesan shavings and chopped basil.

SAVE TIME

Prepare the recipe to the end of step 3. Cover the polenta and sauce and chill separately for up to two days. Complete step 4 to finish the recipe.

Serves 6

Vegetable Tempura

Hands-on time: 20 minutes, plus chilling
Cooking time: 15 minutes

125g (4oz) plain flour, plus 2 tbsp extra
   to sprinkle
2 tbsp cornflour
2 tbsp arrowroot
125g (4oz) cauliflower, cut into
   small florets
2 large carrots, cut into matchsticks
16 button mushrooms
2 courgettes, sliced
2 red peppers, seeded and sliced
vegetable oil to deep-fry
salt and freshly ground black pepper
fresh coriander sprigs to garnish

For the dipping sauce

25g (1oz) fresh root ginger, peeled
   and grated
4 tbsp dry sherry
3 tbsp soy sauce

1 Sift the 125g (4oz) plain flour, the
cornflour and arrowroot into a large
bowl with a pinch each of salt and
ground black pepper. Gradually whisk
in 300ml (½ pint) ice-cold water to
form a thin batter. Cover and chill
in the fridge.

2 To make the dipping sauce, put the
ginger, sherry and soy sauce into a
heatproof bowl and pour 200ml
(7fl oz) boiling water over. Stir well
to mix, then put to one side.

3 Put the vegetables into a large bowl,
sprinkle 2 tbsp flour over them and
toss well to coat. Heat the oil in a wok
or deep-fryer to 170°C (test by frying a
small cube of bread – it should brown
in 40 seconds).

4 Dip a handful of the vegetables in
the batter, then remove with a slotted
spoon, taking up a lot of the batter
with the vegetables. Add to the hot
oil and deep-fry for 3–5 minutes
until crisp and golden. Remove
with a slotted spoon and drain on
kitchen paper; keep them hot while
you cook the remaining batches.
Serve immediately, garnished with
coriander sprigs and accompanied
by the dipping sauce.

Serves 4

Sesame and Cabbage Rolls

Hands-on time: 30 minutes, plus soaking
Cooking time: about 15 minutes, plus cooling

50g (2oz) dried shiitake mushrooms

3 tbsp sesame oil

4 garlic cloves, crushed

4 tbsp sesame seeds

450g (1lb) cabbage, finely shredded

1 bunch of spring onions, chopped

225g can bamboo shoots, drained

3 tbsp soy sauce

½ tsp caster sugar

2 × 270g packs filo pastry

1 large egg, beaten

vegetable oil to deep-fry

Spiced Plum Sauce or Thai Chilli
  Dipping Sauce to serve (see opposite)

1 Put the mushrooms into a heatproof
   bowl and cover with boiling water.
   Soak for 20 minutes.

2 Heat the sesame oil in a wok or large
   frying pan. Add the garlic and sesame
   seeds and fry gently until golden
   brown. Add the cabbage and spring
   onions and fry, stirring, for 3 minutes.

3 Drain and slice the mushrooms. Add
   them to the pan with the bamboo

shoots, soy sauce and sugar and stir
until well mixed. Take the pan off the
heat and leave to cool.

4 Cut the filo pastry into 24 × 18cm (7in)
   squares. Keep the filo squares covered
   with a damp teatowel as you work.
   Place one square of filo pastry on the
   worksurface and cover with a second
   square. Place a heaped tablespoon of
   the cabbage mixture across the centre
   of the top square to within 2.5cm
   (1in) of the ends. Fold the 2.5cm (1in)
   ends of pastry over the filling. Brush
   one unfolded edge of the pastry with
   a little beaten egg, then roll up to
   make a thick parcel shape. Shape the
   remaining pastry and filling in the
   same way to make 12 parcels.

5 Heat a 5cm (2in) depth of oil in a
   deep-fryer or large heavy-based pan
   to 180°C (test by frying a small cube of
   bread – it should brown in 40 seconds).
   Fry the rolls in batches for about
   3 minutes until crisp and golden.
   Remove with a slotted spoon and

drain on kitchen paper; keep them warm while you fry the remainder. Serve hot, accompanied by the dipping sauce.

Spiced Plum Sauce

Slice 2 spring onions as thinly as possible. Put them into a small pan with 6 tbsp plum sauce, the juice of 1 lime, ½ tsp Chinese five-spice powder and 2 tbsp water. Heat gently for 2 minutes.

Thai Chilli Dipping Sauce

Put 200ml (7fl oz) white wine vinegar and 6 tbsp caster sugar into a small pan and bring to the boil, then reduce the heat and simmer for 2 minutes. Add 1 finely chopped red chilli (see Safety Tip, page 29) and 50g (2oz) each finely chopped cucumber, onion and pineapple.

Makes 12

Top 6 Sources of Vegetarian Protein

Pulses

The term 'pulse' is used to describe all the various beans, peas and lentils. Pulses are highly nutritious, especially when eaten with grains such as couscous, pasta, rice or bread. Dried pulses should be stored in airtight containers in a cool, dry cupboard. They keep well, but after about six months their skins start to toughen and they take progressively longer to cook. Most pulses must be soaked prior to cooking. Canned pulses are a convenient, quick alternative to having to soak and cook dried ones, and most supermarkets stock a wide range. A 400g can (drained weight about 235g) is roughly equivalent to 100g (3½oz) dried beans. Dried pulses double in weight after soaking.

Sprouted beans and seeds

These are rich in nutrients and lend a nutty taste and crunchy texture to salads and stir-fries. Fresh bean sprouts are available from most supermarkets. Many beans and seeds can be sprouted at home, although it is important to buy ones that are specifically produced for sprouting – from a health food shop or other reliable source. Mung beans, aduki beans, alfalfa seeds and fenugreek are all suitable.

Cheese

Some vegetarians prefer to avoid cheeses that have been produced by the traditional method, because this uses animal-derived rennet. However, most supermarkets and cheese shops now stock an excellent range of vegetarian cheeses, produced using vegetarian rennet, which comes from plants, such as thistle and mallow, that contain enzymes capable of curdling milk. Always check the label when buying cheese.

Tofu

Also known as bean curd, tofu is made from ground soya beans in a process akin to cheese-making. It is highly nutritious but virtually tasteless. However, it readily absorbs other flavours when marinated.

Tofu is sold as a chilled product and should be stored in the fridge. Once the pack is opened, the tofu should be kept immersed in a bowl of water in the fridge and eaten within four days.

Firm tofu is usually cut into chunks, then immersed in tasty marinades or dressings prior to grilling, stir-frying, deep-frying, adding to stews, or tossing raw into salads. It can also be chopped and made into burgers and nut roasts.

Smoked tofu has more flavour than unsmoked; it is used in the same way but doesn't need marinating.

Silken tofu is softer and creamier than firm tofu and is useful for making sauces and dressings.

Textured vegetable protein (TVP)

TVP forms the bulk of most ready-prepared vegetarian burgers, sausages and mince. It is made from a mixture of soya flour, flavourings and liquid, which is cooked, then extruded under pressure and cut into chunks, or small pieces to resemble mince. It has a slightly chewy, meat-like texture. TVP can be included in stews, pies, curries and other dishes, rather as meat would be used by non-vegetarians.

Quorn

Quorn is a vegetarian product derived from a distant relative of the mushroom. Although it is not suitable for vegans because it contains egg albumen, Quorn is a good source of complete protein for vegetarians. Like tofu, Quorn has a bland flavour and benefits from being marinated before cooking. Find it in the chiller cabinet at the supermarket, and keep it in the fridge.

Stir-fried Beans with Cherry Tomatoes

Hands-on time: 10 minutes
Cooking time: about 8 minutes

350g (12oz) green beans, trimmed

2 tsp olive oil

1 large garlic clove, crushed

150g (5oz) cherry or baby plum tomatoes, halved

2 tbsp freshly chopped flat-leafed parsley

salt and freshly ground black pepper

1 Cook the beans in salted boiling water for 4–5 minutes, then drain well.

2 Heat the oil in a wok or large frying pan over a high heat. Stir-fry the beans with the garlic and tomatoes for 2–3 minutes until the beans are tender and the tomatoes are just beginning to soften without losing their shape. Season well with salt and ground black pepper, then stir in the parsley and serve.

Serves 6

Roasted Ratatouille

Hands-on time: 15 minutes
Cooking time: about 1½ hours

400g (14oz) red peppers, seeded and
   roughly chopped

700g (1½lb) aubergines, cut into chunks

450g (1lb) onions, cut into wedges

4 or 5 garlic cloves, unpeeled and
   left whole

150ml (¼ pint) olive oil

1 tsp fennel seeds

200ml (7fl oz) passata

sea salt and freshly ground black pepper

a few fresh thyme sprigs to garnish

1 Preheat the oven to 240°C (220°C fan oven) mark 9. Put the peppers, aubergines, onions, garlic, oil and fennel seeds into a roasting tin. Season with sea salt flakes and ground black pepper and toss together.

2 Transfer to the oven and cook for 30 minutes (tossing frequently during cooking) or until the vegetables are charred and beginning to soften.

3 Stir the passata through the vegetables and put the roasting tin back in the oven for 50–60 minutes, stirring occasionally. Garnish with the thyme sprigs and serve.

SAVE EFFORT

An easy way to get a brand
new dish is to replace half the
aubergines with 400g (14oz)
courgettes, use a mix of green and
red peppers and garnish with fresh
basil instead of thyme.

Serves 6

Chilli Onions with Goat's Cheese

Hands-on time: 15 minutes
Cooking time: about 45 minutes

75g (3oz) unsalted butter, softened

2 medium red chillies, seeded and finely
chopped (see Safety Tip, opposite)

1 tsp crushed dried chillies

6 small red onions

3 × 100g (3½oz) goat's cheese logs, with
rind (see page 22)

salt and freshly ground black pepper

balsamic vinegar to serve

1 Preheat the oven to 200°C (180°C fan
oven) mark 6. Put the butter into a
small bowl, beat in the fresh and dried
chillies and season well with salt and
ground black pepper.

2 Cut off the root from one of the
onions, sit it on its base, then make
several deep cuts in the top to create a
star shape, slicing about two-thirds of
the way down the onion. Do the same
with the other five onions, then divide
the chilli butter equally among them,
pushing it down into the cuts.

3 Put the onions into a small roasting
tin, cover with foil and bake for 40–45
minutes until soft.

4 About 5 minutes before the onions
are ready, slice each goat's cheese
in two, leaving the rind intact, then
put on a baking sheet and bake for
2–3 minutes.

5 To serve, put each onion on top of a
piece of goat's cheese and drizzle with
balsamic vinegar.

Serves 6

Roasted Root Vegetables

Hands-on time: 15 minutes
Cooking time: about 1 hour

1 large potato, cut into large chunks

1 large sweet potato, cut into large chunks

3 carrots, cut into large chunks

4 small parsnips, halved

1 small swede, cut into large chunks

3 tbsp olive oil

2 fresh rosemary and 2 fresh thyme sprigs

salt and freshly ground black pepper

1 Preheat the oven to 200°C (180°C fan oven) mark 6. Put all the vegetables into a large roasting tin. Add the oil.

2 Use scissors to snip the herbs over the vegetables, then season with salt and ground black pepper and toss everything together. Roast for 1 hour or until tender.

SAVE EFFORT

An easy way to get a brand new dish is to use other combinations of vegetables: try celeriac instead of parsnips, fennel instead of swede, peeled shallots instead of carrots.

Serves 4

Split Pea Roti

Hands-on time: 25 minutes, plus soaking
Cooking time: 40 minutes, plus resting

125g (4oz) yellow split peas, soaked in cold water overnight

¼ tsp ground turmeric

1 tsp ground cumin

1 garlic clove, finely sliced

1½ tsp salt

225g (8oz) plain flour, plus extra to dust

1½ tsp baking powder

1 tbsp vegetable oil, plus extra to fry

125–150ml (4–5fl oz) full-fat milk

vegetable curry to serve

1 Drain the split peas and put them into a small pan with the turmeric, cumin, garlic and 1 tsp of the salt. Add 200ml (7fl oz) cold water and bring to the boil, then reduce the heat and simmer for 30 minutes or until the peas are soft, adding a little more water if necessary. Take off the heat and leave to cool.

2 Sift the flour, baking powder and remaining salt into a large bowl. Make a well in the centre, add the oil and gradually mix in enough milk to form a soft dough. Transfer to a lightly floured worksurface and knead until smooth. Cover with a damp teatowel and leave to rest for 30 minutes.

3 Put the cooled peas into a food processor and blend until smooth, adding 1 tbsp water.

4 Divide the dough into eight. Roll out each piece on a lightly floured surface, to make a 20.5cm (8in) round. Divide the pea mixture between four of the rounds, placing it in the centre of each, then top with the other rounds and press the edges together to seal.

5 Heat a large heavy-based frying pan until really hot. Brush each roti with a little oil and fry (one or two at a time) for 1 minute on each side or until lightly brown. Keep warm while you cook the rest. Serve with a vegetable curry.

Serves 4

Veggie Lunches

Perfect Vitamins and Minerals

Vitamins are vital for proper body functioning. They can be divided into two categories – fat soluble and water soluble. Minerals cannot be manufactured by the body and must be obtained from food.

Vitamins

Fat-soluble vitamins A, D, E and K are found mostly in foods that contain fat. They are stored in the body by the liver. The water-soluble vitamins C and B complex dissolve in water and cannot be stored, so a regular supply is important.

A varied diet should supply all the vitamins our bodies need. Vegetarians and vegans should ensure that their intake of vitamins B12 and D is sufficient, although a deficiency of either is unlikely.

Make the most of vitamins

For maximum vitamin retention, buy fruit and vegetables in peak condition, preferably from a shop with a fast turnover of stock. Eat them as soon as possible. Wilted or old vegetables have a lower vitamin content than fresh.

Store vegetables in a cool, dark place: light is destructive to vitamins, especially vitamins B and C. Don't leave bottles of milk on the doorstep: vitamin B2 (riboflavin) is destroyed when exposed to ultraviolet light.

Steam or boil vegetables until just tender, using the minimum amount of water.

Don't add soda to cooking water. Once vegetables have been cooked and drained, use the water for stocks, gravies and soups.

Don't prepare vegetables hours in advance and leave them soaking in water. Leave the skin on whenever you can.

Eat plenty of raw vegetables and fruit.

Vitamin loss continues after cooking, particularly when warm foods are left waiting around, so eat soon after cooking.

Vitamin B12

Vitamin B12 is essential for the formation of healthy red blood cells; a deficiency causes a form of anaemia. As it is found only in animal foods (with the exception of uncertain amounts in seaweed and fermented soya products), it is the vitamin most likely to be lacking in a vegan diet. Vegetarians who eat milk, eggs and cheese will get sufficient vitamin B12 from these, but vegans should be careful to include some fortified foods in their diet. Yeast extracts, some brands of breakfast cereals, soya milk and other products marketed for vegans (such as vegetable spreads and pâtés) are all good sources. Get into the habit of reading labels to identify fortified brands.

Vitamin D

Vitamin D is needed for the growth and formation of healthy teeth and bones. Most of the body's supply comes from the action of sunlight on the skin. Good vegetarian sources of vitamin D are eggs and butter. Some margarines, milk powders and yogurts are fortified – check the labels.

Minerals

At present, 15 minerals have been identified as being essential to health and others are under investigation. Most people obtain enough minerals provided a good variety of foods is eaten. Iron, calcium and zinc are the three minerals most often discussed in relation to a vegetarian diet.

Iron

Iron is used to make the haemoglobin in red blood cells. Haemoglobin carries oxygen to every cell in the body and a shortage leads to anaemia. Vegetarians are susceptible to anaemia because meat is a rich source of iron, and because the body can absorb iron from meat more efficiently than it can from vegetarian foods. Iron is found in many vegetarian and vegan foods, including leafy green vegetables, cereals, pulses, nuts, eggs and dried fruits (especially apricots). The absorption of iron is greatly increased if vitamin C-rich foods are eaten at the same meal. It is decreased by the presence of tannin, which is found in tea, as well as phytates and oxalates in bran.

Calcium

Calcium is essential for the growth and development of bones and teeth. Because it is usually associated primarily with milk, eggs, yogurt and cheese, vegans are considered to be at risk of deficiency. However, this is not a problem because calcium is also found in white bread and flour, green vegetables, nuts, sesame seeds, dried fruits, calcium-enriched soya milk and tap water in hard-water areas.

Zinc

Zinc is a trace mineral. Among other things, it is important for the functioning of enzymes and for a healthy immune system. It has been suggested that zinc from plant sources is not readily absorbed by the body. However, there are so many other factors that affect zinc absorption and requirements that it is highly unlikely that vegetarianism would be the cause of a deficiency. As long as a variety of food is included in the diet, a deficiency will be avoided. Good vegetarian sources are sesame seeds, cheese, nuts, pulses and grains.

Perfect Couscous

Often mistaken for a grain, couscous is actually a type of pasta that originated in North Africa. It is perfect for serving with stews and casseroles, or making into salads. The tiny pellets do not require any cooking and can simply be soaked.

1 Measure the couscous into a jug and add 1½ times its volume of hot water or stock.
2 Cover the bowl and leave to soak for 5 minutes. Fluff up with a fork before serving.
3 If using for a salad, leave the couscous to cool completely before adding the other salad ingredients.

Perfect Bulgur Wheat

A form of cracked wheat, bulgur has had some or all of the bran removed. It is pre-boiled during manufacturing and may be boiled, steamed or soaked. It is good served as a grain or used in salads.

1 **Simmering bulgur** Cover in water by about 2.5cm (1in). Bring to the boil, then reduce the heat and simmer for 10–15 minutes until just tender. Drain.

2 **Steaming bulgur** Place the bulgur in a steamer lined with a clean teatowel and steam over boiling water for 20 minutes or until the grains are soft.

3 **Soaking bulgur** Put the bulgur into a deep bowl. Cover with hot water and mix with a fork. Leave for 20 minutes, checking to make sure there is enough water. Drain and fluff up with a fork.

1

Summer Couscous

Hands-on time: 10 minutes
Cooking time: 20 minutes

175g (6oz) baby plum tomatoes, halved

2 small aubergines, thickly sliced

2 large yellow peppers, seeded and
  roughly chopped

2 red onions, cut into thin wedges

2 fat garlic cloves, crushed

5 tbsp olive oil

250g (9oz) couscous

400g can chopped tomatoes

2 tbsp harissa paste

25g (1oz) toasted pumpkin seeds
  (optional)

1 large bunch of fresh coriander,
  roughly chopped

salt and freshly ground black pepper

1 Preheat the oven to 230°C (210°C fan oven) mark 8. Put the vegetables and garlic into a large roasting tin, drizzle 3 tbsp of the oil over them and season with salt and ground black pepper. Toss to coat. Roast for 20 minutes or until tender.

2 Meanwhile, put the couscous into a separate roasting tin, add 300ml (½ pint) cold water and leave to soak for 5 minutes. Stir in the tomatoes and harissa and drizzle with the remaining oil. Pop in the oven next to the vegetables for 4–5 minutes to warm through.

3 Stir the pumpkin seeds, if you like, and the coriander into the couscous and season. Add the vegetables and stir through.

Serves 4

Marinated Feta

½ × 200g (7oz) pack feta (see page 22)

1½ tbsp extra virgin olive oil

1 tbsp each freshly chopped dill and mint

grated zest of ¼ orange

salt and freshly ground black pepper

crusty bread and salad to serve

1 Put the feta into a bowl (trying not to break it) and pour the oil over.

2 Scatter the dill, mint and orange zest over it, then season to taste with salt and ground black pepper. Cover and leave to marinate for 1 hour, if you have time.

3 Serve with crusty bread and salad.

Serves 1

Aubergine, Feta and Tomato Stacks

Hands-on time: 10 minutes
Cooking time: 12 minutes

200g (7oz) feta, crumbled (see page 22)

2 tbsp olive oil, plus extra to brush

1 garlic clove, crushed, plus 1 garlic clove to rub

2 plump aubergines, cut into 1cm (½in) thick slices

a handful of fresh basil leaves, torn

3 large vine-ripened tomatoes, each sliced into four

salt and freshly ground black pepper

rocket and toasted ciabatta to serve

SAVE EFFORT

For an easy way to get a brand new dish, replace the feta with sliced mozzarella, or smoked mozzarella. Mix some olive oil with the crushed garlic, brush over the mozzarella and stack up in step 3.

1 Preheat the barbecue or grill. Put the feta into a bowl, stir in the oil and crushed garlic, season with salt and ground black pepper and put to one side.

2 Brush each aubergine slice with a little oil and barbecue or grill for about 6 minutes, turning occasionally, until softened and golden. Take off the heat.

3 Sprinkle a little of the feta mixture on to six of the aubergine slices. Put some torn basil leaves on top and then a slice of tomato. Season well. Repeat with the feta mixture, basil leaves, aubergine and tomato. Finish with a third aubergine slice and press down firmly.

4 Secure each stack with a cocktail stick. Either use a hinged grill rack, well oiled, or wrap the stacks in foil and barbecue for 2–3 minutes on each side. Serve with rocket leaves and toasted ciabatta rubbed with a garlic clove.

Serves 6

Broad Bean and Feta Salad

Hands-on time: 10 minutes
Cooking time: 5 minutes

225g (8oz) podded broad beans (see
  Save Effort)

100g (3½oz) feta, chopped (see page 22)

2 tbsp freshly chopped mint

2 tbsp extra virgin olive oil

a squeeze of lemon juice

salt and freshly ground black pepper

lemon wedges to serve (optional)

1 Cook the beans in salted boiling water
  for 3–5 minutes until tender. Drain,
  then plunge them into cold water and
  drain again. Remove their skins, if you
  like (see Save Effort).

2 Tip the beans into a bowl, add the feta,
  mint, oil and a squeeze of lemon juice.
  Season well with salt and ground
  black pepper and toss together. Serve
  with lemon wedges, if you like.

SAVE EFFORT

For this quantity of broad beans,
you will need to buy about 750g
(1½lb) beans in pods. Choose small
pods, as the beans will be young
and will have a better flavour than
bigger, older beans.

Very young broad beans, less
than 7.5cm (3in) long, can be
cooked in their pods and eaten
whole. Pod older beans and skin
them to remove the outer coat,
which toughens with age. To do
this, slip the beans out of their skins
after blanching. Allow about 250g
(9oz) weight of whole beans in pods
per person.

48

Serves 2

Take 5 Quick Salad Dressings

Blue Cheese

To make 100ml (3½fl oz), you will need:
50g (2oz) Roquefort cheese, 2 tbsp low-fat yogurt, 1 tbsp white wine vinegar, 5 tbsp extra virgin olive oil, salt and freshly ground black pepper.

1 Crumble the cheese into a food processor and add the yogurt, vinegar and oil. Whiz for 1 minute or until thoroughly combined. Season to taste with salt and ground black pepper.
2 If not using immediately, store in a cool place and use within one day.

Chilli Lime

To make 125ml (4fl oz), you will need:
¼ red chilli, seeded and finely chopped (see Safety Tip, page 29), 1 garlic clove, crushed, 1cm (½in) piece fresh root ginger, peeled and finely grated, juice of 1½ large limes, 50ml (2fl oz) olive oil, 1½ tbsp light muscovado sugar, 2 tbsp fresh coriander leaves, 2 tbsp fresh mint leaves.

1 Put the chilli, garlic, ginger, lime juice, oil and sugar into a food processor or blender and whiz for 10 seconds to combine. Add the coriander and mint leaves and whiz together for 5 seconds to chop roughly.
2 If not using immediately, store in a cool place and use within two days.

Mustard

To make about 100ml (3½fl oz), you will need:

1 tbsp wholegrain mustard, juice of ½ lemon, 6 tbsp extra virgin olive oil, salt and freshly ground black pepper.

1 Put the mustard, lemon juice and oil into a small bowl and whisk together. Season to taste with salt and ground black pepper.
2 If not using immediately, store in a cool place and whisk briefly before using.

Lemon and Parsley

To make about 100ml (3½fl oz), you will need:

juice of ½ lemon, 6 tbsp extra virgin olive oil, 4 tbsp freshly chopped flat-leafed parsley, salt and freshly ground black pepper.

1 Put the lemon juice, oil and parsley into a medium bowl and whisk together. Season to taste with salt and ground black pepper.
2 If not using immediately, store in a cool place and whisk briefly before using.

Mint Yogurt

To make about 175ml (6fl oz), you will need:

150g (5oz) Greek yogurt, 3–4 tbsp freshly chopped mint leaves, 2 tbsp extra virgin olive oil, salt and freshly ground black pepper.

1 Put the yogurt into a bowl and add the mint and oil. Season to taste with salt and ground black pepper.
2 If not using immediately, store in a cool place and use within one day.

Goat's Cheese Puff

Hands-on time: 15 minutes
Cooking time: about 25 minutes

50g (2oz) trimmed green beans

¼ × 375g puff pastry block

plain flour to dust

40g (1½oz) soft goat's cheese (see page 22)

1 tbsp freshly chopped mint

beaten egg to glaze

salt and freshly ground black pepper

1 Bring a pan of water to the boil, then add the beans and cook for 3 minutes. Drain, then plunge them into a bowl of ice-cold water. Drain again and pat dry.

2 Preheat the oven to 200°C (180°C fan oven) mark 6. Roll out the pastry on a floured worksurface to make a rough 12.5cm (5in) square. Put the pastry square on a baking sheet.

3 Put the goat's cheese, mint and seasoning to taste in a small bowl and stir to combine. Spread the cheese mixture in a strip diagonally across the pastry, then lay the beans on top of the cheese in a neat bundle. Brush the visible pastry with beaten egg, then fold the two opposite corners over the beans to enclose. Brush the pastry with egg and bake for 15–20 minutes until golden. Serve immediately.

SAVE TIME

Prepare the puff and glaze with the egg (do not cook) up to 2 hours ahead. Chill. Complete the recipe to serve.

Serves 1

Goat's Cheese and Walnut Salad

 Hands-on time: 10 minutes

1 large radicchio, shredded
2 bunches of prepared watercress
  (total weight about 125g/4oz)
1 red onion, finely sliced
150g (5oz) walnut pieces
200g (7oz) goat's cheese, crumbled
  (see page 22)

For the dressing

2 tbsp red wine vinegar
8 tbsp olive oil
a large pinch of caster sugar
salt and freshly ground black pepper

1 Whisk all the ingredients for the dressing together in a small bowl and put to one side.

2 Put the radicchio, watercress and onion into a large bowl. Pour the dressing over and toss well.

3 To serve, divide the salad among six serving plates and sprinkle the walnuts and goat's cheese on top.

Serves 6

Warm Lentil Salad

Hands-on time: 10 minutes
Cooking time: 10 minutes

2 medium eggs
2 tsp olive oil
2 small leeks, trimmed and chopped
4 spring onions, chopped
1 red pepper, seeded and chopped
400g can lentils, drained
150ml (¼ pint) vegetable stock
salt and freshly ground black pepper
a handful of rocket leaves to garnish

1 Gently lower the eggs into a pan of boiling water and simmer for 7 minutes.

2 Meanwhile, heat the oil in a separate pan and fry the leeks, spring onions and red pepper for 6–8 minutes until softened.

3 Stir in the lentils and stock and bring to the boil, then reduce the heat and simmer for 1–2 minutes.

4 Remove the eggs from the pan and, when cool enough to handle, shell them, then cut each in half. Season the lentil mixture with salt and ground black pepper, then divide between two serving bowls and top each with an egg and a few rocket leaves.

Serves 2

Perfect Eggs

Follow these tried and tested steps for perfect poached and boiled eggs.

Poaching

1. Heat about 8cm (3¼in) of lightly salted water in a shallow frying pan to a bare simmer. Crack a very fresh egg into a cup, then slip it into the water. (The whites in a fresh egg are firmer and will form a 'nest' for the yolk, while older egg whites are watery and spread out in the pan.)

2. Cook for 3–4 minutes until the white is barely set. Remove the egg from the water with a slotted spoon and drain on kitchen paper.

Perfect boiled eggs

There are two ways to boil an egg: starting in boiling water or starting in cold water. Both work well as long as you follow certain rules:

- ❏ The egg must be at room temperature
- ❏ For both methods, cover the eggs with water, plus 2.5cm (1in) or so extra
- ❏ If starting in boiling water, use an 'egg pick', if you like, to pierce the broad end of the shell. This allows air in the pocket at the base of the egg to escape and avoids cracking
- ❏ Gently lower the eggs into the pan, using a long spoon to avoid cracking them
- ❏ Cook at a simmer rather than a rolling boil

Boiling

Boiling: method 1

1 Bring a small pan of water to the
   boil. Once the water is boiling,
   lower in a medium egg. For a soft-
   boiled egg, cook for 6 minutes;
   for a salad egg, cook for 8 minutes;
   for a hard-boiled egg, cook for
   10 minutes.
2 Remove the egg from the water
   with a slotted spoon and serve.

Boiling: method 2

1 Lower a medium egg into a small
   pan and cover with cold water.
   Put on a lid and bring to the boil.
   When the water begins to boil,
   remove the lid and cook for
   2 minutes for a soft-boiled egg,
   5 minutes for a salad egg, and
   7 minutes for a hard-boiled egg.
2 Remove the egg from the water
   with a slotted spoon and serve.

1

2

Asparagus and Quail's Egg Salad

Hands-on time: 20 minutes
Cooking time: 4 minutes

24 quail's eggs

24 asparagus spears, trimmed

juice of ½ lemon

5 tbsp olive oil

4 large spring onions, finely sliced

100g (3½oz) watercress,
  roughly chopped

a few fresh dill and tarragon sprigs

salt and freshly ground black pepper

1 Gently lower the quail's eggs into a pan of boiling water and cook for 2 minutes, then drain and plunge them into cold water. Cook the asparagus in salted boiling water for 2 minutes or until just tender. Drain, plunge into cold water and leave to cool.

2 Whisk together the lemon juice and oil and season with salt and ground black pepper. Stir in the spring onions and put to one side.

3 Peel the quail's eggs and cut in half. Put into a large bowl with the asparagus, watercress, dill and tarragon. Pour the dressing over and lightly toss all the ingredients together. Adjust the seasoning and serve.

Serves 8

Avocados

Prepare avocados just before serving because their flesh discolours quickly once exposed to air.

1. Halve the avocado lengthways and twist the two halves apart. Tap the stone with a sharp knife, then twist the knife to remove the stone.
2. Run a knife between the flesh and skin and peel the skin away. Slice the flesh.

Garlic

1 Put the clove on the chopping board and put the flat side of a large knife on top of it. Press down firmly on the flat of the blade to crush the clove and break the papery skin.

2 Cut off the base of the clove and slip the garlic out of its skin. It should come away easily.

3 **Slicing** Using a rocking motion with the knife tip on the board, slice the garlic as thinly as you need.

4 **Shredding and chopping** Holding the slices together, shred them across the slices. Chop the shreds if you need chopped garlic.

5 **Crushing** After step 2, the whole clove can be put into a garlic press. To crush with a knife, roughly chop the peeled cloves and put them on the board with a pinch of salt.

6 **Puréeing** Press down hard with the edge of a large knife tip (with the blade facing away from you), then drag the blade along the garlic while still pressing hard. Continue to do this, dragging the knife tip over the garlic.

Halloumi and Avocado Salad

🍴 **Hands-on time:** 10 minutes
Cooking time: 2 minutes

250g (9oz) halloumi cheese, sliced
   into eight (see Healthy Tip below
   and page 22)

1 tbsp plain flour, seasoned

2 tbsp olive oil

200g (7oz) mixed leaf salad

2 avocados, halved, stoned, peeled
   and sliced

rocket leaves to garnish

lemon halves to serve

For the mint dressing

3 tbsp lemon juice

8 tbsp olive oil

3 tbsp freshly chopped mint

salt and freshly ground black pepper

1 To make the dressing, whisk the
   lemon juice with the oil and mint, then
   season with salt and ground black
   pepper. Put to one side.

2 Coat the halloumi with the flour. Heat
   the oil in a large frying pan and fry
   the cheese for 1 minute on each side or
   until it forms a golden crust.

3 Meanwhile, put the salad leaves and
   avocado into a large bowl, add half the
   dressing and toss together. Arrange
   the hot cheese on top and drizzle the
   remaining dressing over. Garnish
   with rocket leaves and serve with
   lemon halves to squeeze over.

HEALTHY TIP

Halloumi is a firm cheese made
from ewe's milk. It is best used
sliced and cooked.

Serves 4

Warm Salad with Quorn and Berries

Hands-on time: 5 minutes
Cooking time: 12 minutes

2 tbsp olive oil

1 onion, sliced

175g pack Quorn pieces

2 tbsp raspberry vinegar

150g (5oz) blueberries

225g (8oz) mixed salad leaves

salt and freshly ground black pepper

1 Heat the oil in a frying pan, add the onion and cook for 5 minutes or until soft and golden. Increase the heat and add the Quorn pieces. Cook, stirring, for 5 minutes or until golden brown. Season with salt and ground black pepper, then place in a large bowl and put to one side.

2 Add the vinegar, 75ml (3fl oz) water and the blueberries to the frying pan. Bring to the boil and bubble for 1-2 minutes until it reaches a syrupy consistency.

3 Toss the Quorn, blueberry mixture and salad leaves gently together. Serve immediately.

Serves 4

Warm Tofu, Fennel and Bean Salad

Hands-on time: 10 minutes
Cooking time: about 15 minutes

1 tbsp olive oil, plus 1 tsp

1 red onion, finely sliced

1 fennel bulb, finely sliced

1 tbsp cider vinegar

400g can butter beans, drained
and rinsed

2 tbsp freshly chopped flat-leafed parsley

200g (7oz) smoked tofu, sliced
lengthways into eight

salt and freshly ground black pepper

1 Heat the 1 tbsp oil in a large frying pan. Add the onion and fennel and cook over a medium heat for 5–10 minutes. Add the vinegar and heat through for 2 minutes, then stir in the butter beans and parsley. Season with salt and ground black pepper, then tip into a bowl.

2 Add the tofu to the pan with the remaining oil. Cook for 2 minutes on each side or until golden. Divide the bean mixture among four plates and add two slices of tofu to each plate.

Serves 4

Oriental Baked Tofu

Hands-on time: 5 minutes
Cooking time: 15 minutes

150g (5oz) firm tofu

½ garlic clove, thinly sliced

2cm (¾in) piece fresh root ginger,
    peeled and cut into matchsticks

1 tsp soy sauce

a small handful of fresh coriander

a few chilli rings

freshly ground black pepper

lime wedges to serve

1 Preheat the oven to 220°C (200°C fan oven) mark 7. Stack two 30.5cm (12in) sheets of greaseproof paper, baking parchment or foil on top of each other and put the tofu on one side.

2 Sprinkle the garlic slices, ginger, soy sauce and some ground black pepper on top. Fold the paper/parchment/foil over, then fold in the edges to seal.

3 Put the parcel on a baking sheet and cook in the oven for 15 minutes. Open the parcel and sprinkle in the coriander and a few chilli rings. Serve with lime wedges.

SAVE EFFORT

Assemble the parcel and put on a baking sheet (do not cook) up to 3 hours ahead. Chill. Complete the recipe to serve.

Serves 1

Everyday Dishes

Perfect Peppers

Full-flavoured Mediterranean vegetable fruits such as peppers add a rich flavour to many dishes. Some people find pepper skins hard to digest. To peel raw peppers, use a swivel-handled peeler to cut off strips down the length of the pepper. Use a small knife to cut out any parts of the skin that the peeler could not reach.

Seeding peppers

The seeds and white pith of peppers taste bitter, so should be removed.

1   Cut off the top of the pepper, then cut away and discard the seeds and white pith.
2   Alternatively, cut the pepper in half vertically and snap out the white pithy core and seeds. Trim away the rest of the white membrane with a knife.

1

Chargrilling peppers

Charring imparts a smoky flavour and makes peppers easier to peel.

1 Hold the pepper, using tongs, over the gas flame on your hob (or under a preheated grill) until the skin blackens, turning until black all over.

2 Put into a bowl, cover and leave to cool (the steam will help to loosen the skin). Peel.

Spicy Red Pepper Dip

To serve eight, you will need:
3 large red peppers (total weight about 450g/1lb), halved, 200g tub reduced-fat soft cheese, ½ tsp hot pepper sauce.

1 Preheat the grill. Chargrill the peppers as left, then peel and seed.

2 Put the flesh into a food processor or blender with the remaining ingredients and purée until smooth. Cover and leave to chill for at least 2 hours to let the flavours develop. Taste and adjust the seasoning if necessary.

Roasted Stuffed Peppers

Hands-on time: 15 minutes
Cooking time: 55 minutes

40g (1½oz) butter

4 Romano peppers, halved, with stalks on and seeded

3 tbsp olive oil

350g (12oz) chestnut mushrooms, roughly chopped

4 tbsp finely chopped fresh chives

100g (3½oz) feta (see page 22)

50g (2oz) fresh white breadcrumbs

25g (1oz) grated Parmesan (see as above)

salt and freshly ground black pepper

1 Preheat the oven to 180°C (160°C fan oven) mark 4. Use a little of the butter to grease a shallow ovenproof dish and put the peppers in it side by side, ready to be filled.

2 Heat the remaining butter and 1 tbsp of the oil in a pan. Add the mushrooms and fry until golden and no excess liquid is left in the pan. Stir in the chives, then spoon the mixture into the pepper halves.

3 Crumble the feta over the mushrooms. Mix the breadcrumbs and Parmesan in a bowl, then sprinkle over the peppers. Season with salt and ground black pepper and drizzle with the remaining oil.

4 Roast in the oven for 45 minutes or until golden and tender. Serve warm.

Serves 8

Classic Eggs

Follow these tried and tested steps for perfect baked eggs and omelettes.

Baking

You can crack eggs into individual dishes or into a large shallow pan and bake them. They may be cooked on their own, or baked with vegetable accompaniments.

1. Generously smear individual baking dish(es) or one large baking dish with butter.
2. Put in any accompaniments, if using (see Variations and accompaniments, opposite). If using vegetable-based accompaniments, use the back of a spoon to make a hollow or hollows in which to break the egg or eggs. Carefully crack the egg or eggs into the hollows.
3. Bake for 8–10 minutes at 200°C (180°C fan oven) mark 6, or 15–18 minutes at 180°C (160°C fan oven) mark 4 until the whites are set; the yolks should still be quite runny.

Variations and accompaniments

Eggs are delicious baked on a simple bed of sautéed vegetables (such as ratatouille), lightly browned diced potatoes with onions, and also on well-cooked spinach.

Accompaniments must be fully cooked before they are transferred to the dish and the raw eggs put on top.

Other simple additions include freshly chopped herbs.

If you like, drizzle a small spoonful of cream and a good grinding of black pepper on top of the eggs before baking.

Perfect omelettes

- ❑ Don't add butter until the pan is already hot, otherwise it will brown too much
- ❑ Beat the eggs lightly
- ❑ Use a high heat

Classic omelette

1 To make an omelette for one person, heat a heavy-based 18cm (7in) frying pan or omelette pan. Using a fork, beat 2 eggs and season with salt and freshly ground black pepper.

2 Add 15g (½oz) butter to the pan and let it sizzle for a few moments without browning, then pour in the eggs and stir a few times with a fork.

3 As the omelette begins to stick at the sides, lift it up and allow the uncooked egg to run into the gap.

4 When the omelette is nearly set and the underneath is brown, loosen the edges and give the pan a sharp shake to slide the omelette across.

5 Add a filling (such as grated cheese or fried mushrooms), if you like, and fold the far side of the omelette towards you. Tilt the pan to slide the omelette on to the plate and serve.

Deluxe Baked Eggs

Hands-on time: 5 minutes
Cooking time: about 12 minutes

15g (½oz) butter
100g (3½oz) sliced chestnut mushrooms
1 tbsp brandy (optional)
leaves from 1 fresh thyme sprig
rocket leaves
2 medium eggs
salt and freshly ground black pepper

1 Preheat the grill. Heat the butter over a high heat in a small frying pan, then cook the mushrooms for 5 minutes or until tender. Add the brandy, if you like, and the thyme leaves and cook for 1 minute, then season well and put to one side.

2 Next, put some rocket leaves in the bottom of a shallow, individual ovenproof serving dish, then top with the mushroom mixture. Crack in the eggs, garnish with a few more thyme leaves and season.

3 Grill for 5 minutes or until the eggs are set. Serve immediately.

SAVE TIME

Prepare the mushroom mixture in step 1 up to 2 hours ahead. Keep at room temperature. Complete steps 2 and 3 to finish the recipe.

Serves 1

Quorn Lasagne

Hands-on time: 15 minutes
Cooking time: about 1 hour

3 tbsp olive oil

1 onion, finely chopped

2 × 300g bags frozen Quorn mince

100ml (3½fl oz) red wine

2 × 400g cans chopped tomatoes

1½ tbsp mixed dried herbs

½ vegetable stock cube

4 tbsp plain flour

600ml (1 pint) milk

9 'no need to pre-cook' lasagne sheets

50g (2oz) mature Cheddar, grated (see page 22)

salt and freshly ground black pepper

green salad to serve

1 Heat 1 tbsp of the oil in a large pan and fry the onion for 10 minutes or until softened. Turn up the heat, add the Quorn and fry for 5 minutes or until golden. Add the wine and simmer for 5 minutes.

2 Stir in the tomatoes and mixed herbs, then crumble in the stock cube and seasoning to taste. Bring the mixture to the boil, then reduce the heat and simmer for 5 minutes or until thickened. Take off the heat.

3 Next, make the white sauce. Heat the remaining oil in a small pan and stir in the flour. Cook for 30 seconds, then take the pan off the heat and gradually whisk in the milk. Put the milk mixture back on to the heat and bring to the boil, then reduce the heat and simmer for 5 minutes, whisking constantly, or until thickened and glossy.

4 Preheat the oven to 200°C (180°C fan oven) mark 6. Spoon a third of the mince mixture into the bottom of a 2 litre (3½ pint) ovenproof dish. Cover with three lasagne sheets and a little white sauce. Repeat the layering process twice more, finishing with a layer of white sauce. Sprinkle the cheese over and cook for 30–35 minutes until bubbling and golden (cover with foil if browning too quickly). Serve immediately with a green salad.

Serves 6

Cherry Tomato and Goat's Cheese Tart

Hands-on time: 10 minutes
Cooking time: about 25 minutes

320g sheet ready-rolled puff pastry

125g (4oz) soft goat's cheese (see page 22)

1 tsp caster sugar

300g (11oz) cherry tomatoes, halved

1 tbsp balsamic vinegar

1 tbsp extra virgin olive oil

salt and freshly ground black pepper

a small handful of fresh basil leaves, torn, to garnish

green salad to serve

1 Preheat the oven to 220°C (200°C fan oven) mark 7. Line a baking tray with greaseproof paper.

2 Unroll the pastry sheet on to the prepared baking tray. Crumble or spread the cheese over the pastry, leaving a 1cm (½in) border around the edge. Sprinkle half the sugar over the cheese, then arrange the tomatoes on top, cut side up. Season well, then sprinkle the remaining sugar over.

3 Cook the tart in the oven for 25 minutes or until the pastry is golden and risen. Remove from the oven and drizzle with the vinegar and oil, then garnish with torn basil leaves. Serve warm or at room temperature with a green salad.

Lentil Chilli

Hands-on time: 15 minutes
Cooking time: about 25 minutes

1 tbsp vegetable oil

1 red onion, finely chopped

1 tsp each ground cumin, coriander and
chilli powder

2 × 400g cans chopped tomatoes

1 vegetable stock cube, crumbled

2 × 400g cans lentils, drained and rinsed

400g can kidney beans, drained
and rinsed

a handful of fresh coriander, chopped

salt and freshly ground black pepper

crisp flatbreads or boiled brown rice
to serve

1 Heat the oil in a large pan and fry the onion for 10 minutes or until soft. Add the ground spices and cook for a further minute. Stir in the tomatoes, stock cube and lentils and simmer for 10 minutes or until thickened.

2 Add the kidney beans and heat through. Stir through most of the coriander and check the seasoning. Garnish with the remaining coriander and serve with crisp flatbreads or boiled brown rice.

Perfect Barley

There are three types of barley, all of which may
be cooked on their own, or in a soup or stew.

Barley

1 **Whole barley** Soak the barley
overnight in twice its volume of
water, then drain well. Put the
barley into a heavy-based pan,
pour boiling water over and
simmer for about 1½ hours until
tender. Check the liquid, adding
more if necessary.

2 **Scotch (pot) barley** Rinse
well, then simmer gently in
boiling water for 45–50 minutes
until tender.

3 **Pearl barley** This barley has had
all of its outer husk removed and
needs no soaking. Rinse the barley
and put it into a pan with twice its
volume of water. Bring to the boil,
then reduce the heat and simmer
until tender – 25–30 minutes.

Perfect Quinoa

Quinoa is a nutritious South American grain,
which makes a great alternative to rice.

Quinoa

1   Put the quinoa into a bowl of
cold water. Mix well, then soak for
2 minutes and drain. Put into a
large pan with twice its volume
of water.

2   Bring to the boil, then reduce the
heat and simmer for 20 minutes.
Remove from the heat, cover
with the lid and leave to stand
for 10 minutes.

Veggie Barley Risotto

Hands-on time: 10 minutes
Cooking time: about 45 minutes

1 tbsp extra virgin olive oil

1 large onion, finely chopped

300g (11oz) pearl barley

50ml (2fl oz) white wine

1.3 litres (2¼ pints) hot vegetable stock

1 tbsp tapenade

½ small head broccoli, cut into small florets

200g (7oz) frozen peas

a small handful of rocket

salt and freshly ground black pepper

grated Parmesan to serve (optional, see page 22)

1 Heat the oil in a large pan over a medium heat. Fry the onion for 10 minutes or until soft. Stir in the barley and fry for 1 minute. Pour in the wine and bring to the boil, then reduce the heat and simmer, stirring, for 2 minutes.

2 Gradually add the hot stock, stirring well after each addition and adding the next ladleful only when the previous one has been absorbed. Continue until the barley is cooked – about 30 minutes, but you don't need to stir all the time and might not need all the stock.

3 Stir the tapenade through, then add the broccoli and peas and cook for 3 minutes more. Season, then stir the rocket through and serve topped with grated cheese, if you like.

Serves 4

Perfect Aubergines

Aubergines are in season from summer into autumn and range in colour from dark purple-black through to lilac and cream. They can be stored in the fridge for up to two weeks.

Cutting aubergines

1 Trim the aubergine to remove the stalk and end.
2 **Slicing** Cut the aubergine into slices as thick as the pieces you will need for your recipe.
3 **Cutting and dicing** Stack the slices and cut across them to the appropriate size for fingers. Cut again in the opposite direction for dice.

Stuffing aubergines

1. To hollow out an aubergine for stuffing, cut off the stalk and halve the aubergine lengthways.
2. Make deep incisions in the flesh, using a crisscross pattern, being careful not to pierce the skin.
3. Using a spoon, scoop out the flesh, leaving the skin intact, and use according to your recipe.

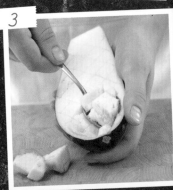

Stuffed Aubergines

Hands-on time: 10 minutes, plus standing
Cooking time: 30 minutes

4 small aubergines

2 tbsp olive oil

25g (1oz) butter

1 small onion, very finely chopped

peeled 4 small ripe tomatoes, and roughly chopped

2 tsp chopped fresh basil or 1 tsp dried

2 medium eggs, hard-boiled and roughly chopped

1 tbsp capers

225g (8oz) fontina or Gruyère, sliced (see page 22)

salt and ground black pepper

herby couscous to serve

1 Cut the aubergines in half lengthways and scoop out the flesh. Put the aubergine shells to one side.

2 Chop the aubergine flesh finely, then spread out on a plate and sprinkle with salt. Leave to stand for 20 minutes (this removes the bitter flavour), then turn into a colander. Rinse, drain and dry.

3 Preheat the oven to 180°C (160°C fan oven) mark 4. Heat half the oil in a frying pan with the butter add the onion and fry gently for 5 minutes until soft but not coloured. Add the tomatoes, basil and salt and ground black pepper to taste.

4 Meanwhile, put the aubergine shells in a single layer in an oiled ovenproof dish. Brush the insides with the remaining oil, then bake for 10 minutes.

5 Spoon half the tomato mixture into the aubergine shells. Cover with a layer of egg, capers, then a layer of cheese. Spoon the remaining tomato mixture over the top. Bake for a further 15 minutes and serve sizzling hot with herby couscous.

Serves 4

Aubergine and Tomato Bake

Hands-on time: 15 minutes
Cooking time: about 35 minutes

1 tbsp olive oil

1 large onion, finely crushed

2 garlic cloves, crushed

2 × 400g cans chopped tomatoes

150g (5oz) quinoa

1 tbsp tomato purée

a large handful of fresh basil, chopped

2 medium aubergines, cut into
 medium chunks

50g (2oz) Parmesan, grated (see page 22)

salt and freshly ground black pepper

1 Heat half the oil in a large pan over a medium heat and fry the onion gently for 10 minutes or until softened. Add the garlic for the last 2 minutes.

2 Add the tomatoes, quinoa, tomato purée and 300ml (½ pint) just-boiled water and simmer for 20 minutes or until the quinoa is tender. Stir most of the basil through and check the seasoning.

3 Meanwhile, heat the remaining oil in a separate pan and fry the aubergines for 15 minutes or until softened – add a splash of water if the pan looks dry.

4 Preheat the grill to medium. Empty the quinoa mixture into a 2 litre (3½ pint) ovenproof dish. Top with the aubergines, then sprinkle the Parmesan over. Grill for 3–5 minutes until piping hot and golden. Garnish with the remaining basil and serve immediately.

Serves 4

Spiced Bean and Vegetable Stew

Slow Cooker Recipe

Hands-on time: 15 minutes
Cooking time: about 10 minutes in pan, then about 3 hours on Low

3 tbsp olive oil

2 small onions, sliced

2 garlic cloves, crushed

1 tbsp sweet paprika

1 small dried red chilli, seeded and finely chopped

700g (1½lb) sweet potatoes, cubed

700g (1½lb) pumpkin, cut into chunks

125g (4oz) okra, trimmed

500g jar passata

400g can haricot or cannellini beans, drained and rinsed

450ml (¾ pint) hot vegetable stock

salt and freshly ground black pepper

1 Heat the oil in a large pan over a very gentle heat. Add the onions and garlic and cook for 5 minutes.

2 Stir in the paprika and chilli and cook for 2 minutes, then add the sweet potatoes, pumpkin, okra, passata, beans and hot stock. Season generously with salt and ground black pepper and bring to the boil.

3 Transfer to the slow cooker, cover and cook on Low for 2–3 hours until the vegetables are tender.

SAVE EFFORT

An easy way to get a brand new dish is to use 1 tsp each ground cumin and ground coriander instead of the paprika. Garnish with freshly chopped coriander.

Serves 6

Veggie Bean Burgers

Hands-on time: 15 minutes
Cooking time: about 10 minutes

349g pack firm tofu

2½ tbsp korma curry paste (see Healthy Tip)

4 spring onions, roughly chopped

a small handful of fresh parsley, roughly chopped

1 tsp paprika

1½ × 410g cans black-eyed beans, drained and rinsed

50g (2oz) fresh white breadcrumbs

½ tbsp oil

salt and freshly ground black pepper

salad to serve

1 Preheat the grill to medium and set the rack 10cm (4in) away from the heat source. Put the tofu, curry paste, spring onions, parsley, paprika and lots of seasoning into a food processor. Whiz until just combined, but not smooth. Add the beans and pulse briefly until they are roughly broken up. Tip the mixture into a large bowl.

2 Using your hands, add the breadcrumbs, then shape the mixture into four equal patties (squeezing together well). Transfer the patties to a baking sheet, brush with the oil and grill for 7–10 minutes until golden on top and piping hot. Serve immediately with a salad.

HEALTHY TIP

Check the ingredients in the curry paste: some may not be suitable for vegetarians.

SAVE EFFORT

If you can't find korma paste, any curry paste will do.

Serves 4

Veggie Curry

Hands-on time: 5 minutes
Cooking time: 12 minutes

1 tbsp medium curry paste (see Healthy Tip, page 100)

227g can chopped tomatoes

150ml (¼ pint) hot vegetable stock

200g (7oz) vegetables, such as broccoli, courgettes and sugarsnap peas, roughly chopped

½ × 400g can chickpeas, drained and rinsed

griddled wholemeal pitta bread and yogurt to serve

1 Heat the curry paste in a large heavy-based pan for 1 minute, stirring the paste to warm the spices. Add the tomatoes and hot stock and bring to the boil, then reduce the heat to a simmer and add the vegetables. Simmer for 5–6 minutes until the vegetables are tender.

2 Stir in the chickpeas and heat for 1–2 minutes until hot. Serve the vegetable curry with a griddled wholemeal pitta and yogurt.

Food for Friends and Family

The Vegetarian Family

Whether your family are already committed vegetarians or are thinking of giving up meat and fish altogether, it is essential that everyone gets a good balanced diet.

Vegetarian children

From the age of one, your child should be eating (or at least be offered) three small meals a day, along with a mid-morning and a mid-afternoon snack (which could be a glass of milk, some chopped fruit or a piece of cheese). From the age of two, your child can eat much the same as the rest of the family. Avoid nuts unless they are ground into nut butter because there is danger of choking. The Department of Health advises that children should not be given soft-cooked eggs. So make sure that poached eggs are cooked until the yolk is set, and avoid giving children soft scrambled eggs and runny omelettes.

Feeding a vegetarian teenager

Adolescents need a nutrient-rich diet with lots of calories (girls about 2,100, boys about 2,800 per day). A varied vegetarian diet will easily provide this. Teenage girls should ensure they eat plenty of iron-rich foods. Encourage them to eat vitamin C and iron-rich foods together (see page 38). Vegan adolescents should eat cereals and yeast extracts fortified with vitamin B12 (see page 37).

For some families, a non-meat-eater in their midst can cause problems at meal times. It's important to view this as a positive move for the family as a whole rather than as a problem. There's no doubt that the consumption of too much animal protein is unhealthy, so it's a good idea to use the opportunity to introduce more meat-free meals to all members of the household. Making meals based on rice, potatoes and pasta is a good way to start. It's easy to cook simple nutritious vegetarian meals using these as a base combined with beans, lentils and well-flavoured ingredients such as garlic, tomato, spices, herbs and fresh vegetables. Tasty risottos, pilafs, vegetable gratins and stuffed baked potatoes are delicious and would usually be made without meat anyway. For particularly steadfast carnivorous members of the family, serve these with grilled meat or fish or sliced cold meat as a last resort until the appeal of vegetarianism sinks in.

Pizzas are surprisingly quick and easy to make and are loved by most teenagers. Piled high with vegetables and served with a large mixed salad, they make a splendid supper. A chunky soup made from a mixture of vegetables and beans or lentils, served with hot garlic bread and followed by yogurt and fruit also makes a healthy meal.

Meat substitutes such as Quorn, and soya products like soya mince are useful additions to the new vegetarian cook's repertoire. Use them to make meat-free versions of traditional family favourites such as shepherd's pie, lasagne, spaghetti bolognese, kebabs and curry.

Vegetarian Pea Pithivier

Hands-on time: 30 minutes, plus chilling
Cooking time: about 55 minutes, plus cooling

175g (6oz) frozen peas

½ tbsp olive oil

2 onions, finely sliced

175g (6oz) full-fat cream cheese (see page 22)

a small handful of fresh parsley, finely chopped

½ tbsp wholegrain mustard

1 tbsp freshly chopped tarragon

40g (1½oz) fresh white breadcrumbs

plain flour to dust

500g pack puff pastry

1 medium egg, lightly beaten

salt and freshly ground black pepper

SAVE TIME

Prepare the pithivier to the end of step 3 up to one day ahead. To serve, reglaze with beaten egg and complete the recipe.

1 Take the peas out of the freezer and put to one side. Heat the oil in a medium pan and cook the onions gently for 10–15 minutes until soft. Empty into a large bowl and cool.

2 Stir the cream cheese, parsley, mustard, tarragon, breadcrumbs, peas and plenty of seasoning into the cooled onion bowl.

3 Lightly flour a worksurface and roll out one-third of the pastry until it is 3mm (⅛in) thick. Cut out a 20.5cm (8in) pastry circle and put on a baking tray. Spoon the pea mixture on to the circle and, leaving a 3cm (1¼in) border of pastry around the edge, shape the filling into a flattened disc with straight edges, about 3cm (1¼in) tall. Brush the border around the filling with beaten egg. Next, roll out the remaining pastry as before, until it is 3mm (⅛in) thick. Place it over the filling, then smooth it down to get rid of any air bubbles. Press down firmly on the edges to seal, then trim into a

neat circle (using the base circle as a guide). Crimp the edges. Brush with beaten egg, then score the top lightly in a pattern like the spokes of a wheel. Chill for at least 1 hour.

4 Preheat the oven to 200°C (180°C fan oven) mark 6 and put a separate baking tray in the oven to heat up. Working quickly and carefully, transfer the prepared pithivier on to the hot baking tray and cook in the oven for 30-40 minutes until deep golden. Serve warm or at room temperature.

Serves 6

Jarlsberg and Sweet Onion Tart

Hands-on time: 20 minutes
Cooking time: about 1 hour

plain flour to dust

375g (13oz) shortcrust pastry

1 tbsp olive oil

2 large onions, finely sliced

1 tsp caster sugar

150g (5oz) Jarlsberg cheese, finely cubed
(see page 22)

3 medium eggs

200ml (7fl oz) double cream

2 tbsp freshly chopped chives or parsley

salt and freshly ground black pepper

green salad to serve

1 Preheat the oven to 200°C (180°C fan oven) mark 6. Lightly dust a worksurface with flour and roll out the pastry large enough to line a 20.5cm (8in) round, 4cm (1½in) deep, fluted tart tin. Prick the base all over with a fork.

2 Line the pastry with a sheet of baking parchment or greaseproof paper and fill with baking beans. Put the tin on a baking tray and bake blind for 15–20 minutes until the pastry sides are set.

3 While the pastry is cooking, heat the oil in a large pan and cook the onions gently for 15–20 minutes, covered, until very soft. Stir in the sugar, turn up the heat and cook, stirring frequently, until the onions are lightly caramelised. Put to one side.

4 Carefully remove the parchment and baking beans from the tin and put the pastry back into the oven. Cook for a further 10 minutes or until the base is cooked through and feels sandy to the touch. Take the tin out of the oven and reduce the oven temperature to 170°C (150°C fan oven) mark 3.

5 Spoon the onions on to the pastry base and dot the cheese over. Put the eggs into a large jug and beat lightly, then mix in the cream, herbs and plenty of seasoning. Pour over the onions and cook in the oven for 25–30 minutes until set and lightly golden. Serve warm or at room temperature with a green salad.

Serves 6

Veggie Risotto Cakes

Hands-on time: about 35 minutes
Cooking time: about 50 minutes, plus cooling

3 tbsp olive oil

1 medium onion, finely chopped

375g (13oz) risotto (arborio) rice

75ml (3fl oz) white wine (optional)

1.1 litres (2 pints) hot vegetable stock

125g (4oz) fine asparagus, chopped into pea-size pieces

125g (4oz) frozen peas

finely grated zest of 1 lemon

50g (2oz) baby spinach leaves

8 medium eggs

salt and freshly ground black pepper

1 tbsp freshly chopped chives to garnish (optional)

salad to serve

1 Heat 1 tbsp of the oil in a large pan and fry the onion gently for 10 minutes or until softened. Stir in the rice and cook for 1 minute. Add the wine, if you like, and simmer for 1 minute.

2 Gradually add the hot stock, stirring well after each addition and adding the next ladleful only when the previous one has been absorbed. Continue until the rice is cooked – about 20 minutes.

3 When the risotto is 2 minutes away from being ready, stir in the asparagus, peas, lemon zest and spinach. When the rice is tender, check the seasoning, then empty on to a large clean tray. Flatten the mixture (this will help the rice to cool quickly) and leave to cool completely.

4 Shape the mixture into eight equal patties.

5 Heat the remaining oil in a large non-stick pan and cook the cakes for 10 minutes, turning once, until golden and hot.

6 Meanwhile, bring a medium pan of water to the boil. Crack an egg into a coffee cup or ramekin. Swirl the water to create a 'whirlpool', then carefully tip in the egg. Crack another egg into the cup and add to the water. Simmer the eggs for 3–4 minutes until the whites are set and the yolks remain

soft – lift an egg out with a slotted spoon and gently prod with your finger to check. Transfer the cooked eggs to a shallow dish of warm water. Repeat with the remaining eggs.

7 Top each risotto cake with a drained poached egg. Season, sprinkle with chopped chives, if you like, and serve with salad.

FREEZE AHEAD

To make ahead and freeze, prepare the risotto cakes to the end of step 4, then arrange on a baking tray lined with baking parchment. Open freeze until solid, then transfer to a sealable container or bag for two months. To serve, thaw in the fridge overnight, or using the defrost setting of a microwave. Complete steps 5, 6 and 7 to finish the recipe.

Makes 8

Baked Stuffed Pumpkin

Hands-on time: about 30 minutes
Cooking time: about 1¾ hours, plus standing

1 pumpkin (weight about 1.4–1.8kg/3–4lb)

2 tbsp olive oil

2 leeks, trimmed and chopped

2 garlic cloves, crushed

2 tbsp freshly chopped thyme leaves

2 tsp paprika

1 tsp ground turmeric

125g (4oz) long-grain rice, cooked

2 tomatoes, peeled, seeded and diced

50g (2oz) cashew nuts, toasted and roughly chopped

125g (4oz) Cheddar, grated (see page 22)

salt and freshly ground black pepper

1 Cut a 5cm (2in) slice from the top of the pumpkin and put to one side for the lid. Scoop out and discard the seeds. Using a knife and a spoon, cut out most of the pumpkin flesh, leaving a thin shell. Cut the pumpkin flesh into small pieces and put to one side.

2 Heat the oil in a large pan, add the leeks, garlic, thyme, paprika and turmeric and fry for 10 minutes. Add the chopped pumpkin flesh and fry for a further 10 minutes or until golden, stirring frequently to prevent sticking. Transfer the mixture to a bowl. Preheat the oven to 180°C (160°C fan oven) mark 4.

3 Add the pumpkin mixture to the cooked rice along with the tomatoes, cashews and cheese. Fork through to mix and season with salt and ground black pepper.

4 Spoon the stuffing mixture into the pumpkin shell, top with the lid and cook in the oven for 1¼–1½ hours until the pumpkin is softened and the skin is browned. Remove from the oven and leave to stand for 10 minutes. Cut into wedges to serve.

Tomato Tarte Tatin

Hands-on time: 25 minutes
Cooking time: about 1 hour 10 minutes

½ tbsp olive oil

3 red onions, finely sliced

2 fresh thyme sprigs, leaves only, plus extra to garnish

50g (2oz) caster sugar

a small knob of butter

½ tbsp balsamic vinegar

650g (1lb 7oz) plum tomatoes, halved

375g pack ready-rolled puff pastry

green salad to serve

1 Heat the oil in a large pan, add the onions, cover and cook gently for 15 minutes. Take off the lid, turn up the heat and cook, stirring, for 5 minutes or until the onions begin to caramelise. Stir in the thyme leaves and put to one side.

2 Preheat the oven to 220°C (200°C fan oven) mark 7. Put a heavy-based 24cm (9½in) round casserole dish or ovenproof frying pan over a low heat. Add the sugar and 50ml (2fl oz) water and heat gently, stirring, until the sugar dissolves, then turn up the heat and allow the sugar to caramelise (do not stir, just swirl the pan occasionally). When the sugar is deeply caramelised (it should be the colour of honey), carefully add the butter and vinegar – it will spit and hiss. Stir to combine, then take the pan off the heat.

3 Arrange the tomatoes, cut side down, in a single layer in the bottom of the casserole or pan. Cover with the cooked onions. Unroll the pastry and cut out a circle 1cm (½in) larger than the bottom of the casserole or pan (it's fine to use trimmings to make a complete circle). Position the pastry on top of the onions and tuck in the edges.

4 Cook in the oven for 30–40 minutes until the pastry is deep golden. Take out of the oven and leave to rest for 5 minutes. Invert on to a plate, garnish with thyme leaves and serve with a green salad.

Serves 4

Mushroom Roulade

Hands-on time: 20 minutes
Cooking time: about 20 minutes

250g (9oz) frozen spinach, thawed

4 large eggs, separated

freshly grated nutmeg

3½ tbsp cornflour

15g (½oz) butter

2 shallots, finely sliced

350g (12oz) mushrooms, sliced

400ml (14fl oz) skimmed milk

25g (1oz) mature Cheddar, grated (see page 22)

1 tsp English mustard

salt and freshly ground black pepper

green salad to serve

1 Preheat the oven to 190°C (170°C fan oven) mark 5. Line a 30.5 × 23cm (12 × 9in) tin with baking parchment. Squeeze out as much moisture as you can from the thawed spinach and put it into a large bowl. Stir in the egg yolks, nutmeg and plenty of seasoning.

2 Put the egg whites into a separate clean grease-free bowl and whisk until they hold stiff peaks. Quickly beat in 1½ tbsp of the cornflour, then fold the mixture into the spinach bowl. Empty on to the prepared tin, spreading it to the corners, then cook for 12–15 minutes until golden and firm to the touch.

3 Heat the butter in a large frying pan and cook the shallots for 5 minutes or until softened. Turn up the heat and add the mushrooms. Cook for 8–10 minutes until softened and any water in the pan has evaporated. Stir in the remaining cornflour, then the milk and heat, stirring, until thickened. Stir in the cheese and mustard. Check the seasoning.

4 Take the spinach base out of the oven and transfer with the paper to a board. Slide a palette knife underneath the roulade to loosen, if necessary, then spread the mushroom mixture over the top. Roll up lengthways as neatly as you can (don't worry if there's some spillage) and serve warm in slices with a green salad.

Serves 6

Cooking Polenta

This classic Italian staple, made of ground cornmeal, may be cooked to make a grainy purée to be served immediately, or cooled and then fried or grilled.

Traditional polenta

1. Fill a pan with 1.1 litres (2 pints) water and add ¼ tsp salt. Pour in 225g (8oz) polenta and put the pan over a medium heat.

2. As the water starts to heat up, stir the polenta. Bring to the boil, then reduce the heat to a simmer and continue cooking, stirring every few minutes, for 15–20 minutes until it comes away from the sides of the pan.

Perfect polenta

- ❑ Use coarse cornmeal if you want a slightly gritty texture, or fine cornmeal for a smooth texture
- ❑ If you are serving traditional polenta straight from the pan, have all the other dishes ready – the polenta needs to be eaten straight away, otherwise it becomes thick and difficult to serve

Grilling polenta

1 Make traditional polenta (see opposite), then pour into an oiled baking dish. Smooth the surface with a spatula and leave to cool.
2 Cut the polenta into squares and brush the pieces with olive oil.
3 Preheat the grill or frying pan and cook for 5–10 minutes until hot and browned on both sides.

Baking polenta

1 Preheat the oven to 200°C (180°C fan oven) mark 6. Fill a pan with 1.1 litres (2 pints) water and add ¼ tsp salt. Pour in 225g (8oz) polenta and put it over the heat. Bring to the boil, stirring, then reduce the heat and simmer for 5 minutes.
2 Pour the polenta into an oiled baking dish, cover with foil and bake in the oven for 45–50 minutes. Brown under the grill.

Griddled Polenta and Ratatouille Stack

🍴 **Hands-on time:** 30 minutes
Cooking time: about 55 minutes, plus cooling

1 tbsp olive oil, plus extra to grease
and drizzle

1 red onion, finely chopped

2 courgettes (total weight about
400g/14oz), finely diced

1 aubergine, finely diced

1 green pepper, finely diced

1 large garlic clove, finely chopped

2 × 400g cans chopped tomatoes

a large pinch of sugar

750ml (1¼ pints) strong vegetable stock

175g (6oz) instant dry polenta

75g (3oz) mature Cheddar, finely grated
(see page 22)

4 medium eggs

a large handful of fresh basil leaves, torn

salt and freshly ground black pepper

crisp green salad to serve

1 Heat the oil in a large pan and fry the
onion gently for 10 minutes or until
soft. Turn up the heat to medium
and add the courgettes, aubergine
and green pepper, then fry for 8–10
minutes until lightly coloured. Stir in
the garlic, tomatoes and sugar and
simmer for 10–15 minutes until thick
and pulpy.

2 Meanwhile, line a rough 22 × 30.5cm
(8½ × 12in) baking tray with baking
parchment. Pour the stock into a large
pan and bring to the boil, then stir
in the polenta. Reduce the heat and
simmer hard for 5 minutes, stirring
continuously (take care – it may
bubble volcanically), until the mixture
thickens. Stir in the cheese and lots
of seasoning, then tip the mixture
on to the prepared tray and spread
to the edges to make an even 1cm
(½in) thick layer. Leave to cool for 10
minutes or until set.

3 Cut the polenta into 12 equal squares.
Grease a griddle pan really well,
then heat over a high heat until it is
smoking hot. Add a few of the polenta

122

squares and fry for 4 minutes until griddle lines appear, then flip over and cook for a further 4 minutes on the other side. Grease the pan well between batches, and cook the remainder of the polenta squares in the same way.

4 Meanwhile, bring a medium pan of water to the boil. Crack an egg into a cup or ramekin. Swirl the water to create a 'whirlpool', then carefully tip in the egg. Crack another egg into the cup and add to the water. Reduce the heat and simmer for 3–4 minutes until the whites are set and the yolks soft – lift an egg out with a slotted spoon and gently prod with your finger to check. Transfer the cooked eggs to a shallow dish of warm water. Repeat with the remaining eggs.

5 Stir the basil into the ratatouille and season to taste. To assemble each serving, layer up three polenta squares with ratatouille between them, then top with a poached egg. Drizzle a little olive oil over and sprinkle with plenty of ground black pepper. Serve with a crisp green salad.

Serves 4

Broccoli, Gorgonzola and Walnut Quiche

Hands-on time: 10 minutes, plus chilling
Cooking time: about 1 hour

400g (14oz) shortcrust pastry

plain flour to dust

150g (5oz) broccoli florets

100g (3½oz) crumbled gorgonzola (see page 22)

2 medium eggs

1 medium egg yolk

300ml (½ pint) double cream

25g (1oz) roughly chopped walnut halves

salt and freshly ground black pepper

1 Preheat the oven to 200°C (180°C fan oven) mark 6. Roll out the pastry on a floured worksurface until the thickness of a £1 coin, then use to line a 23 × 2.5cm (9 × 1in) deep fluted tart tin. Prick the base all over and chill for 15 minutes. Cover the pastry with greaseproof paper and fill with baking beans. Bake blind for 15 minutes, then remove the beans and paper and bake for a further 5 minutes or until the base is dry and light golden. Reduce the oven temperature to 150°C (130°C fan oven) mark 2.

2 Cook the broccoli in boiling water for 3 minutes, then drain and dry on kitchen paper. Arrange the broccoli in the pastry case. Dot with the gorgonzola. Whisk together the eggs, egg yolk, cream and some seasoning, then pour into the case. Scatter the walnut halves over and cook the quiche for 40 minutes or until the filling is set. Serve warm or at room temperature.

Serves 6

Red Onion Tarte Tatin

Hands-on time: 15 minutes
Cooking time: about 40 minutes, plus cooling

50g (2oz) butter

2 tbsp olive oil

1.1kg (2½lb) red onions, sliced into rounds

1 tbsp light muscovado sugar

175ml (6fl oz) white wine

4 tsp white wine vinegar

1 tbsp freshly chopped thyme, plus extra to garnish (optional)

450g (1lb) puff pastry

plain flour to dust

salt and freshly ground black pepper

1 Lightly grease two 23cm (9in) non-stick sandwich tins with a little of the butter and put to one side.

2 Melt the remaining butter with the oil in a large non-stick frying pan. Add the onions and sugar and fry for 10–15 minutes until golden, keeping the onions in their rounds.

3 Preheat the oven to 220°C (200°C fan oven) mark 7. Add the wine, vinegar and thyme to the pan, then bring to the boil and let it bubble until the liquid has evaporated. Season with salt and ground black pepper, then divide the mixture between the tins and leave to cool.

4 Halve the pastry. Roll out each piece thinly on a lightly floured worksurface into a round shape just larger than the sandwich tin. Put one pastry round over the onion mixture in each tin and tuck in the edges. Prick the pastry dough all over with a fork.

5 Cook the tarts in the oven for 15–20 minutes until the pastry is risen and golden. Take out of the oven and put a large warm plate over the pastry. Turn the whole thing over and shake gently to release the tart, then remove the tin. Scatter with thyme, if you like, and cut into wedges to serve.

SAVE TIME

Prepare the tarte tatin to the end of
step 4. Cover and keep in the fridge
for up to 24 hours. Complete step
5 to finish the recipe.

Serves 12

Comfort Food

Mushroom and Bean Hotpot

Hands-on time: 15 minutes
Cooking time: 45 minutes

3 tbsp olive oil

700g (1½lb) chestnut mushrooms, roughly chopped

1 large onion, finely chopped

2 tbsp plain flour

2 tbsp mild curry paste (see Healthy Tip, page 100)

150ml (¼ pint) dry white wine

400g can chopped tomatoes

2 tbsp sun-dried tomato paste

2 × 400g cans mixed beans, drained and rinsed

3 tbsp mango chutney

3 tbsp roughly chopped fresh coriander and mint

1 Heat the oil in a large pan over a low heat, then fry the mushrooms and onion until the onion is soft and dark golden. Stir in the flour and curry paste and cook for 1–2 minutes.

2 Add the wine, tomatoes, tomato paste and beans and bring to the boil, then reduce the heat and simmer gently for 30 minutes or until most of the liquid has reduced. Stir in the chutney and herbs before serving.

Easy Leek Pie

Hands-on time: 15 minutes
Cooking time: 1 hour

275g (10oz) plain flour, plus extra to dust
1 tsp English mustard powder
175g (6oz) cold butter, cut into cubes
50g (2oz) mature Cheddar, grated
(see page 22)
2 medium egg yolks, lightly beaten
900g (2lb) leeks, trimmed and cut into
1cm (½in) slices, washed and drained
2 medium red onions, each cut into
8 wedges
juice of ½ lemon
leaves of 5 fresh thyme sprigs
4 tbsp olive oil
1 small egg, lightly beaten
salt and freshly ground black pepper
seasonal vegetables to serve

1 Put the flour, mustard powder, butter
and ½ tsp salt into a food processor
and pulse until the mixture forms
crumbs. Add the cheese, egg yolks
and 2–3 tbsp cold water and process
briefly until the mixture comes
together, then form into a ball, wrap in
clingfilm and put into the freezer for
10 minutes.

2 Preheat the oven to 200°C (180°C fan
oven) mark 6. Cook the leeks with
3 tbsp water in a covered pan until
softened. Drain and put to one side.
Gently cook the onions and lemon
juice in a covered pan until softened.

3 Roll out the pastry on a large, lightly
floured sheet of baking parchment,
to a 38cm (15in) round. Lift the paper
and pastry on to a baking sheet. Put
the onions and leeks in the centre of
the pastry, leaving a 7.5cm (3in) border
around the edge. Sprinkle with the
thyme, season with salt and ground
black pepper and drizzle with the oil.
Fold the pastry edges over the filling
and brush the pastry rim with beaten
egg. Cook in the oven for 50 minutes
or until the vegetables are tender.
Serve with seasonal vegetables.

Moroccan Chickpea Stew

Hands-on time: 10 minutes
Cooking time: about 40 minutes

1 red pepper, halved and seeded

1 green pepper, halved and seeded

1 yellow pepper, halved and seeded

2 tbsp olive oil

1 onion, finely sliced

2 garlic cloves, crushed

1 tbsp harissa paste

2 tbsp tomato purée

½ tsp ground cumin

1 aubergine, diced

400g can chickpeas, drained and rinsed

450ml (¾ pint) vegetable stock

4 tbsp roughly chopped fresh flat-leafed parsley, plus a few sprigs to garnish

salt and freshly ground black pepper

crusty bread to serve

1 Preheat the grill and lay the peppers, skin side up, on a baking sheet. Grill for about 5 minutes until the skins begin to blister and char. Put the peppers into a plastic bag, seal and put to one side for a few minutes. When cooled a little, peel off the skins and discard, then slice the peppers and put to one side.

2 Heat the oil in a large heavy-based frying pan over a low heat, add the onion and cook for 5–10 minutes until soft. Add the garlic, harissa, tomato purée and cumin and cook for 2 minutes.

3 Add the peppers to the pan with the aubergine. Stir everything to coat evenly with the spices and cook for 2 minutes. Add the chickpeas and stock, season well with salt and ground black pepper and bring to the boil. Reduce the heat and simmer for 20 minutes.

4 Just before serving, stir the chopped parsley through the chickpea stew. Garnish with parsley sprigs and serve with crusty bread.

Mixed Mushroom Cannelloni

🍴 **Hands-on time:** 15 minutes
Cooking time: about 1 hour

6 sheets fresh lasagne

3 tbsp olive oil

1 small onion, finely sliced

3 garlic cloves, sliced

20g pack fresh thyme, finely chopped

225g (8oz) chestnut or brown-cap
  mushrooms, roughly chopped

125g (4oz) flat-cap mushrooms,
  roughly chopped

2 × 125g goat's cheese logs, with rind (see
  page 22)

350g carton cheese sauce (see as above)

salt and freshly ground black pepper

green salad to serve

SAVE EFFORT

Fresh lasagne sheets wrapped
around a filling are used here to
make cannelloni, but you can also
buy cannelloni tubes, which can
easily be filled using a teaspoon.

1 Preheat the oven to 180°C (160°C fan
  oven) mark 4. Cook the lasagne in
  boiling water until just tender. Drain
  well, then run it under cold water to
  cool. Keep covered with cold water
  until ready to use.

2 Heat the oil in a large pan and add the
  onion. Cook over a medium heat for
  7–10 minutes until the onion is soft.
  Add the garlic and fry for 1–2 minutes.
  Keep a few slices of garlic to one side.
  Keep a little thyme for sprinkling
  later, then add the rest to the pan with
  the mushrooms. Cook for a further 5
  minutes or until the mushrooms are
  golden brown and there is no excess
  liquid in the pan. Season, remove from
  the heat and put to one side.

3 Crumble one of the goat's cheese logs
  into the cooled mushroom mixture
  and stir together. Drain the lasagne
  sheets and pat dry with kitchen paper.
  Spoon 2–3 tbsp of the mushroom
  mixture along the long edge of each
  lasagne sheet, leaving a 1cm (½in)

border around the edge. Roll up the pasta sheets and cut each roll in half. Put the pasta into a shallow ovenproof dish and spoon the cheese sauce over it. Slice the remaining goat's cheese into thick rounds and arrange across the middle of the pasta rolls. Sprinkle the reserved garlic and thyme on top.

4 Cook in the oven for 30–35 minutes until golden and bubbling. Serve with a green salad.

Serves 4

Butternut Squash and Spinach Lasagne

Hands-on time: 20 minutes
Cooking time: about 1 hour

1 butternut squash, peeled, halved,
    seeded and cut into 3cm (1¼in) cubes

2 tbsp olive oil

1 onion, sliced

25g (1oz) butter

25g (1oz) plain flour

600ml (1 pint) milk

250g (9oz) ricotta (see page 22)

1 tsp freshly grated nutmeg

225g bag baby leaf spinach

6 'no need to pre-cook' lasagne sheets

50g (2oz) pecorino cheese or Parmesan,
    grated (see as above)

salt and freshly ground black pepper

1 Preheat the oven to 200°C (180°C fan oven) mark 6. Put the squash into a roasting tin with the oil, onion and 1 tbsp water. Mix well and season with salt and ground black pepper. Roast in the oven for 25 minutes, tossing halfway through.

2 To make the sauce, melt the butter in a pan, then stir in the flour and cook over a medium heat for 1–2 minutes. Gradually add the milk, stirring constantly. Reduce the heat to a simmer and cook, stirring, for 5 minutes or until the sauce has thickened. Crumble the ricotta into the sauce and add the nutmeg. Mix together thoroughly and season with salt and ground black pepper.

3 Heat 1 tbsp water in a pan. Add the spinach, cover and cook until just wilted. Season generously.

4 Spoon the squash mixture into a 1.7 litre (3 pint) ovenproof dish. Layer the spinach on top, then cover with a third of the sauce, then the lasagne. Spoon the remaining sauce on top, season and sprinkle with the grated cheese. Cook for 30–35 minutes until the cheese topping is golden and the pasta is cooked.

Perfect Pasta

Perfectly cooked pasta can be a super-quick accompaniment or a meal in itself. Whether you are cooking dried or fresh pasta, follow these simple steps, then add an easy pasta sauce for a meal in minutes.

Cooking pasta

There are a number of mistaken ideas about cooking pasta, such as adding oil to the water, adding salt only at a certain point, and rinsing the pasta after cooking. The basics couldn't be simpler. Filled pasta is the only type of pasta that needs oil in the cooking water – the oil reduces friction, which could tear the wrappers and allow the filling to come out. Use 1 tbsp for a large pan of water. Rinse pasta after cooking only if you are going to cool it to use in a salad.

Dried pasta

1 Heat the water with about 1 tsp salt per 100g (3½oz) of pasta. Bring to a rolling boil, then add all the pasta and stir well for 30 seconds, to keep the pasta from sticking.
2 Once the water is boiling again, set the timer for 2 minutes less than the cooking time on the pack and cook uncovered.
3 Check the pasta when the timer goes off, then every 60 seconds until it is cooked al dente: tender, but with a slight bite at the centre. Drain in a colander. The pasta will continue to cook a little after draining.

Fresh pasta

Fresh pasta is cooked in the same way as dried, but for a shorter time. Bring the water to the boil. Add the pasta to the boiling water all at once and stir well. Set the timer for 2 minutes and keep testing every 30 seconds until the pasta is cooked al dente: tender, but with a slight bite at the centre. Drain in a colander. The pasta will continue to cook a little after draining.

Perfect Rice

There are two main types of rice: long-grain and short-grain. Long-grain rice is generally served as an accompaniment, while short-grain rice is used for dishes such as risotto, sushi and paella. Long-grain rice needs no special preparation, although basmati should be washed to remove excess starch.

Basmati rice

Put the rice into a bowl and cover with cold water. Stir until this becomes cloudy, then drain and repeat until the water is clear. Soak the rice for 30 minutes, then drain before cooking.

Long-grain rice

1 Use 50–75g (2–3oz) raw rice per person; measured by volume 50–75ml (2–2½fl oz). Measure the rice by volume and put it into a pan with a pinch of salt and twice the volume of boiling water (or stock).

2 Bring to the boil, then reduce the heat to low and set the timer for the time stated on the pack. The rice should be al dente: tender with a slight bite at the centre.

3 When the rice is cooked, fluff up the grains with a fork.

Pappardelle with Spinach

Hands-on time: 5 minutes
Cooking time: 12 minutes

350g (12oz) pappardelle pasta

350g (12oz) baby leaf spinach, roughly chopped

2 tbsp olive oil

75g (3oz) ricotta (see page 22)

freshly grated nutmeg

salt and freshly ground black pepper

1 Cook the pappardelle in a large pan of lightly salted boiling water according to the pack instructions until al dente. Drain the pasta well.

2 Put the pasta back into the pan and add the spinach, oil and ricotta, tossing for 10–15 seconds until the spinach has wilted. Season with a little nutmeg, salt and ground black pepper and serve immediately.

Serves 4

Pesto Gnocchi

TAKE 5

Hands-on time: 10 minutes
Cooking time: 10 minutes

800g (1lb 12oz) fresh gnocchi

200g (7oz) green beans, trimmed
  and chopped

125g (4oz) fresh pesto (see page 22)

10 sunblush tomatoes, roughly chopped

salt

1 Cook the gnocchi in a large pan of lightly salted boiling water according to the pack instructions or until all the gnocchi have floated to the surface. Add the beans to the water for the last 3 minutes of cooking time.

2 Drain the gnocchi and beans and put back into the pan. Add the pesto and tomatoes and toss well. Serve immediately.

Serves 4

Pasta with Goat's Cheese and Sunblush Tomatoes

Hands-on time: 5 minutes
Cooking time: 10 minutes

300g (11oz) conchiglie pasta

2 tbsp olive oil

1 red pepper, seeded and chopped

1 yellow pepper, seeded and chopped

½ tbsp sun-dried tomato paste

75g (3oz) sunblush tomatoes

75g (3oz) soft goat's cheese (see page 22)

2 tbsp freshly chopped parsley

salt and freshly ground black pepper

1 Cook the pasta in a large pan of lightly salted boiling water according to the pack instructions until al dente.

2 Meanwhile, heat the oil in a pan and fry the red and yellow peppers for 5–7 minutes until softened and just beginning to brown. Add the tomato paste and cook for a further minute. Add a ladleful of pasta cooking water to the pan and simmer for 1–2 minutes to make a sauce.

3 Drain the pasta and put back into the pan. Pour the sauce on top, then add the tomatoes, goat's cheese and parsley. Toss together until the cheese begins to melt, then season with ground black pepper and serve.

Serves 4

Asparagus Risotto

Hands-on time: 10 minutes
Cooking time: about 30 minutes

50g (2oz) butter

2 shallots, diced

2 garlic cloves, crushed

225g (8oz) risotto (arborio) rice

500ml (18fl oz) hot vegetable stock

2 tbsp mascarpone

50g (2oz) Parmesan, finely grated, plus shavings to garnish (see page 22)

2 tbsp freshly chopped parsley

400g (14oz) asparagus spears, blanched and halved

1 Melt the butter in a heavy-based pan, add the shallots and garlic and cook over a gentle heat until soft.

2 Stir in the rice and cook for 1–2 minutes, then add the hot stock. Bring to the boil, then reduce the heat and simmer for 15–20 minutes, stirring occasionally to ensure that the rice isn't sticking, until almost all the stock has been absorbed and the rice is tender.

3 Add the mascarpone, half the Parmesan and half the parsley to the pan. Stir in the asparagus and the remaining parsley and Parmesan. Divide among four plates, garnish with shavings of Parmesan and serve.

Serves 4

Delicious
Desserts

Sticky Banoffee Pies

🍴 **Hands-on time:** 15 minutes, plus chilling

150g (5oz) digestive biscuits

75g (3oz) unsalted butter, melted, plus extra to grease

1 tsp ground ginger (optional)

450g (1lb) dulce de leche toffee sauce

4 bananas, peeled, sliced and tossed in the juice of 1 lemon

300ml (½ pint) double cream, lightly whipped

plain chocolate shavings

1 Put the biscuits into a food processor and whiz until they resemble fine crumbs. (Alternatively, put them into a plastic bag and crush with a rolling pin.) Transfer to a bowl. Add the melted butter and ginger, if you like, then process, or stir well, for 1 minute to combine.

2 Butter six 10cm (4in) rings or tartlet tins and line with greaseproof paper. Press the biscuit mixture evenly into the bottom of each ring. Divide the toffee sauce equally among the rings and top with the bananas. Pipe or spoon on the cream, sprinkle with chocolate shavings and chill.

3 Remove from the rings or tins to serve.

SAVE MONEY

Slightly overripe bananas are ideal for this recipe.

Serves 6

Fruity Rice Pudding

Hands-on time: 10 minutes, plus chilling
Cooking time: 1 hour, plus cooling

125g (4oz) pudding rice

1.1 litres (2 pints) full-fat milk

1 tsp vanilla extract

3–4 tbsp caster sugar

200ml (7fl oz) whipping cream

6 tbsp wild lingonberry sauce to serve

1 Put the rice into a pan with 600ml (1 pint) cold water and bring to the boil, then reduce the heat and simmer until the liquid has evaporated. Add the milk and bring to the boil, then reduce the heat and simmer for 45 minutes or until the rice is very soft and creamy. Leave to cool.

2 Add the vanilla extract and sugar to the rice. Lightly whip the cream and fold through the pudding. Chill in the fridge for 1 hour.

3 Divide the rice mixture among six glass dishes and top with 1 tbsp lingonberry sauce.

SAVE EFFORT

Although wild lingonberry sauce is used here, a spoonful of any fruit sauce or compote, such as strawberry or blueberry, will taste delicious.

For an easy alternative presentation, serve in tumblers, layering the rice pudding with the fruit sauce; you will need to use double the amount of fruit sauce.

Serves 6

Pear and Blackberry Crumble

Hands-on time: 20 minutes
Cooking time: about 45 minutes

450g (1lb) pears, peeled, cored and
    chopped, tossed with the juice of
    1 lemon

100g (3½oz) golden caster sugar

1 tsp mixed spice

450g (1lb) blackberries

cream, vanilla custard or ice cream
    to serve

For the crumble topping

100g (3½oz) butter, chopped, plus
    extra to grease

225g (8oz) plain flour

75g (3oz) ground almonds

125g (4oz) golden caster sugar

1 Put the pears and lemon juice into a
    bowl, add the sugar and mixed spice,
    then add the blackberries and toss
    thoroughly to coat.

2 Preheat the oven to 200°C (180°C fan
    oven) mark 6. Lightly butter a 1.8 litre
    (3¼ pint) shallow ovenproof dish, then
    carefully tip the fruit into the dish in an
    even layer.

3 To make the topping, put the butter,
    flour, ground almonds and sugar
    into a food processor and pulse until
    the mixture begins to resemble
    breadcrumbs. Tip into a bowl.
    (Alternatively, rub the butter into the
    flour in a large bowl by hand or using
    a pastry cutter. Stir in the ground
    almonds and sugar.) Bring parts of the
    mixture together with your hands to
    make lumps.

4 Spoon the crumble topping evenly
    over the fruit, then bake for 35–45
    minutes until the fruit is tender and the
    crumble is golden and bubbling. Serve
    with cream, custard or ice cream.

- A versatile recipe that can be popped in the oven while you whip up your main course
- Make double the amount of crumble topping and freeze half for an easy pudding another day

- An easy way to get a brand new dish is to replace the pears with apples, or omit the blackberries and use 700g (1½lb) plums or rhubarb instead. You could also use gooseberries (omit the spice), or try 450g (1lb) rhubarb with 450g (1lb) strawberries

Serves 6

Quick Gooey Chocolate Puddings

Hands-on time: 15 minutes
Cooking time: about 20 minutes

100g (3½oz) unsalted butter, plus extra to grease

100g (3½oz) golden caster sugar, plus extra to dust

100g (3½oz) plain chocolate (at least 70% cocoa solids), broken into pieces

2 large eggs

20g (¾oz) plain flour

icing sugar to dust

1 Preheat the oven to 200°C (180°C fan oven) mark 6. Butter four 200ml (7fl oz) ramekins and dust with sugar. Melt the chocolate and butter in a heatproof bowl over a pan of gently simmering water, making sure the base of the bowl doesn't touch the water. Take the bowl off the pan and leave to cool for 5 minutes.

2 Whisk the eggs, caster sugar and flour together in a bowl until smooth. Fold in the chocolate mixture and pour into the prepared ramekins.

3 Stand the dishes on a baking tray and bake for 12–15 minutes until the puddings are puffed and set on the outside, but still runny inside.

4 Turn out, dust with icing sugar and serve immediately.

Serves 4

Maple Pecan Pie

Hands-on time: 40 minutes, plus chilling
Cooking time: 1¼ hours

250g (9oz) plain flour, sifted

a large pinch of salt

225g (8oz) unsalted butter, cubed
and chilled

100g (3½oz) light muscovado sugar

125g (4oz) dates, stoned and
roughly chopped

grated zest and juice of ½ lemon

100ml (3½fl oz) maple syrup, plus
6 tbsp extra

1 tsp vanilla extract

4 medium eggs

300g (11oz) pecan nut halves

300ml (½ pint) double cream

2 tbsp bourbon whiskey

SAVE EFFORT

An easy way to get a brand
new dish is to replace the lemon
with orange, the pecans with
walnut halves and the whiskey
with Cointreau.

1 Put the flour and salt into a food processor. Add 125g (4oz) of the butter and whiz to fine crumbs, then add 2 tbsp water and whiz until the mixture just comes together. Wrap in clingfilm and chill for 30 minutes. Use to line a 28 × 4cm (11 × 1½in) loose-bottomed tart tin, then cover and chill for 30 minutes. Preheat the oven to 200°C (180°C fan oven) mark 6.

2 Prick the pastry all over, cover with greaseproof paper and fill with baking beans. Bake blind for 25 minutes, then remove the beans and paper and bake for a further 5 minutes or until the base is dry and light golden.

3 Meanwhile, whiz the rest of the butter in a food processor to soften. Add the sugar and dates and whiz to cream together. Add the lemon zest and juice, the 100ml (3½fl oz) maple syrup, the vanilla extract, eggs and 200g (7oz) of the nuts. Whiz until the nuts are finely chopped – the mixture

will look curdled, but don't worry. Pour into the pastry case and top with the rest of the nuts.

4 Bake for 40–45 minutes until almost set in the middle. Cover with greaseproof paper for the last 10 minutes if the nuts turn very dark. Cool slightly before removing from the tin, then brush with 4 tbsp maple syrup. Lightly whip the cream with the whiskey and 2 tbsp maple syrup, then serve with the pie.

Serves 10

Baked Raspberry Meringue Pie

TAKE 5

🍴 **Hands-on time:** 15 minutes
Cooking time: about 8 minutes

8 trifle sponges

450g (1lb) raspberries, lightly crushed

2–3 tbsp raspberry liqueur

3 medium egg whites

150g (5oz) golden caster sugar

1 Preheat the oven to 230°C (210°C fan oven) mark 8. Put the trifle sponges in the bottom of a 2 litre (3½ pint) ovenproof dish. Spread the raspberries on top and drizzle with the raspberry liqueur.

2 Whisk the egg whites in a clean grease-free bowl until stiff peaks form. Gradually whisk in the sugar until the mixture is smooth and glossy. Spoon the meringue mixture over the raspberries and bake for 6–8 minutes until golden.

SAVE EFFORT

If you don't have any raspberry liqueur, you can use another fruit-based liqueur such as Grand Marnier instead.

162

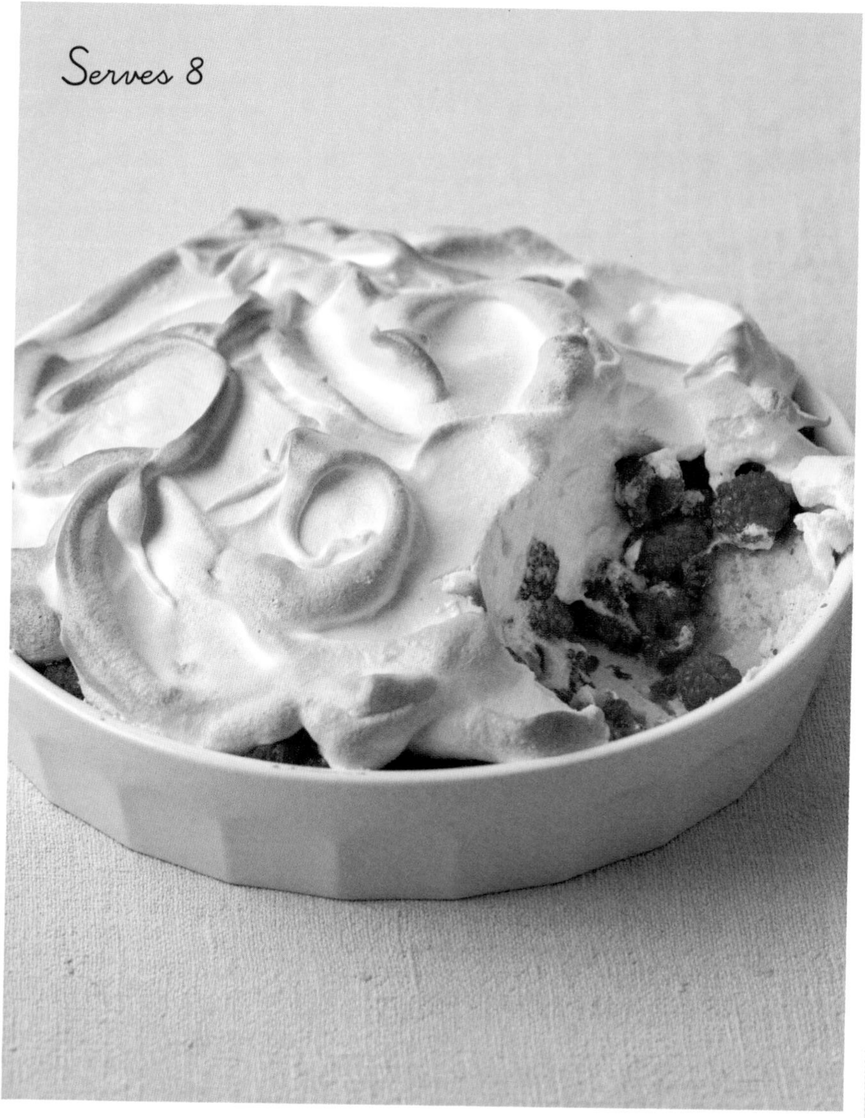
Serves 8

Strawberry Brûlée

Hands-on time: 15 minutes, plus chilling
Cooking time: 5 minutes

250g (9oz) strawberries, hulled
and sliced

2 tsp golden icing sugar

1 vanilla pod

400g (14oz) Greek yogurt

100g (3½oz) golden caster sugar

1 Divide the strawberries among
   four ramekins and sprinkle with
   icing sugar.

2 Scrape the seeds from the vanilla pod
   and stir into the yogurt, then spread
   the mixture evenly over the fruit.

3 Preheat the grill to high. Sprinkle the
   caster sugar evenly over the yogurt
   until it's well covered.

4 Put the ramekins on a baking sheet
   or into the grill pan and grill until
   the sugar turns dark brown and
   caramelises. Leave for 15 minutes
   or until the caramel is cool enough to
   eat, or chill in the fridge for up to
   2 hours before serving.

SAVE EFFORT

An easy way to get a brand
new dish is to use raspberries
or blueberries instead of the
strawberries.

Serves 4

Tropical Fruit and Coconut Trifle

Hands-on time: 30 minutes, plus chilling

1 small pineapple, roughly chopped

2 bananas, thickly sliced

2 × 400g cans mango slices in syrup, drained, syrup put to one side

2 passion fruit, halved

175g (6oz) plain sponge, such as Madeira cake, roughly chopped

3 tbsp dark rum (optional)

200ml (7fl oz) coconut cream

500g carton fresh custard

500g carton Greek yogurt

600ml (1 pint) double cream

6 tbsp dark muscovado sugar

1 Put the pineapple pieces into a large trifle bowl, add the banana and mango slices and spoon the passion fruit pulp over them. Top with the chopped sponge, then pour on the rum, if you like, and 6 tbsp of the reserved mango syrup.

2 Mix the coconut cream with the custard and pour the mixture over the sponge.

3 Put the yogurt and cream into a bowl and whisk until thick. Spoon or pipe the mixture over the custard, then sprinkle with the sugar. Cover and chill for at least 1 hour before serving.

SAVE TIME

Complete the recipe, then cover and chill for up to two days.

Serves 16

Summer Pudding

Hands-on time: 10 minutes, plus overnight chilling
Cooking time: 10 minutes

800g (1lb 12oz) mixed summer berries, such as 250g (9oz) each redcurrants and blackcurrants and 300g (11oz) raspberries

125g (4oz) golden caster sugar

3 tbsp crème de cassis

9 thick slices slightly stale white bread, crusts removed

crème fraîche or clotted cream to serve (optional)

1 Put the redcurrants and blackcurrants into a medium pan. Add the sugar and cassis and bring to a simmer, then cook for 3–5 minutes until the sugar has dissolved. Add the raspberries and cook for 2 minutes. Once the fruit is cooked, taste it – there should be a good balance between tart and sweet.

2 Meanwhile, line a 1 litre (1¾ pint) bowl with clingfilm. Put the base of the bowl on one piece of bread and cut around it. Put the circle of bread in the bottom of the bowl.

3 Line the inside of the bowl with more slices of bread, slightly overlapping them to prevent any gaps. Spoon in the fruit, making sure the juice soaks into the bread. Keep back a few spoonfuls of juice in case the bread is unevenly soaked when you turn out the pudding.

4 Cut the remaining bread to fit the top of the pudding neatly, using a sharp knife to trim any excess bread from around the edges. Wrap in clingfilm, weigh down with a saucer and a can and chill overnight.

5 To serve, unwrap the outer clingfilm, upturn the pudding on to a plate and remove the inner clingfilm. Drizzle with the reserved juice and serve with crème fraîche or clotted cream, if you like.

Serves 8

216 cal ♥ 3g protein
9g fat (3g sat) ♥ 2g fibre
31g carb ♥ 1.5g salt

246 cal ♥ 9g protein
9g fat (3g sat) ♥ 3g fibre
32g carb ♥ 1g salt

249 cal ♥ 10g protein
9g fat (4g sat) ♥ 1g fibre
31g carb ♥ 0.9g salt

450 cal ♥ 7g protein
21g fat (3g sat) ♥ 5g fibre
55g carb ♥ 2.1g salt

251 cal ♥ 4g protein
10g fat (1g sat) ♥ 9g fibre
39g carb ♥ 0.2g salt

429 cal ♥ 13g protein
14g fat (2g sat) ♥ 4g fibre
65g carb ♥ 1.3g salt

405 cal ♥ 8g protein
21g fat (3g sat) ♥ 5g fibre
49g carb ♥ 0g salt

Calorie Gallery

428 cal ♥ 12g protein
41g fat (10g sat) ♥ 2g fibre
3g carb ♥ 0.5g salt

300 cal ♥ 23g protein
10g fat (2g sat) ♥ 9g fibre
33g carb ♥ 0.5g salt

127 cal ♥ 7g protein
11g fat (2g sat) ♥ 2g fibre
1g carb ♥ 0.1g salt

189 cal ♥ 5g protein
14g fat (6g sat) ♥ 2g fibre
11g carb ♥ 0.9g salt

321 cal ♥ 16g protein
25g fat (11g sat) ♥ 1g fibre
0.5g carb ♥ 0.4g salt

539 cal ♥ 36g protein
19g fat (5g sat) ♥ 8g fibre
58g carb ♥ 2.5g salt

485 cal ♥ 12g protein
33g fat (17g sat) ♥ 0.8g fibre
27g carb ♥ 1.5g salt

10

12

16

18

30

32

42

54

58

60

76

80

82

84

per roll: 224 cal
7g protein ♥ 13g fat
(2g sat) ♥ 3g fibre
23g carb ♥ 0.7g salt

236 cal ♥ 3g protein
19g fat (3g sat) ♥ 5g fibre
14g carb ♥ 0.5g salt

276 cal ♥ 11g protein
23g fat (16g sat) ♥ 0.8g fibre
5g carb ♥ 0.9g salt

30 cal ♥ 1g protein
1.5g fat (trace sat)
2g fibre ♥ 3g carb ♥ 0g salt

24

26

28

403 cal ♥ 16g protein
7g fat (16g sat)♥ 0g fibre
2g carb ♥ 3.5g salt

138 cal ♥ 6g protein
11g fat (5g sat) ♥ 2g fibre
4g carb ♥ 1.2g salt

197 cal ♥ 14g protein
16g fat (4g sat) ♥ 7g fibre
5g carb ♥ 1.3g salt

496 cal ♥ 15g protein
34g fat (8g sat) ♥ 1g fibre
35g carb ♥ 1.3g salt

46

48

52

397 cal ♥ 13g protein
4g fat (13g sat) ♥ 3g fibre
11g carb ♥ 2.3g salt

152 cal ♥ 7g protein
7g fat (1g sat) ♥ 4g fibre
15g carb ♥ 0.3g salt

113 cal ♥ 12g protein
6g fat (1g sat) ♥ 3g fibre
1g carb ♥ 0.1g salt

150 cal ♥ 9g protein
6g fat (1g sat)♥ 5g fibre
15g carb ♥ 0.8g salt

66

68

70

307 cal ♥ 21g protein
5g fat (1g sat) ♥ 3g fibre
48g carb ♥ 1.0g salt

386 cal ♥ 12g protein
6g fat (1g sat) ♥ 4g fibre
72g carb ♥ 1.5g salt

404 cal ♥ 21g protein
33g fat (17g sat) ♥ 5g fibre
6g carb ♥ 1.0g salt

240 cal ♥ 22g protein
9g fat (3g sat) ♥ 4g fibre
2g carb ♥ 1.5g salt

6

90

94

96

262 cal ♥ 7g protein
7g fat (1g sat) ♥ 8g fibre
44g carb ♥ 1.3g salt

98

278 cal ♥ 19g protein
8g fat (1g sat) ♥ 4g fibre
34g carb ♥ 0.7g salt

100

468 cal ♥ 22g protein
20g fat (3g sat) ♥ 13g fibre
58g carb ♥ 1.4g salt

102

569 cal ♥ 10g protein
39g fat (21g sat)♥ 3g fibre
36g carb ♥ 1.0g salt

108

Calorie Gallery

163 cal ♥ 11g protein
8g fat (4g sat) ♥ 3g fibre
11g carb ♥ 0.5g salt

118

427 cal ♥ 21g protein
18g fat (6g sat)♥ 6g fibre
46g carb ♥ 0.7g salt

122

683 cal ♥ 12g protein
57g fat (27g sat) ♥ 2g fibre
33g carb ♥ 1.5g salt

124

631 cal ♥ 26g protein
37g fat (18g sat) ♥ 2g fibre
50g carb ♥ 1.9g salt

136

273 cal ♥ 15g protein
17g fat (7g sat) ♥ 3g fibre
18g carb ♥ 0.6g salt

138

404 cal ♥ 14g protein
11g fat (3g sat) ♥ 4g fibre
67g carb ♥ 0.3g salt

142

323 cal ♥ 7g protein
17g fat (10g sat) ♥ 0.1g fibre
36g carb ♥ 0.2g salt

154

525 cal ♥ 7g protein
21g fat (9g sat) ♥ 6g fibre
81g carb ♥ 0.3g salt

156

468 cal ♥ 5g protein
31g fat (19g sat) ♥ 0.6g fibre
46g carb ♥ 0.6g salt

158

748 cal ♥ 9g protein
57g fat (24g sat)♥ 3g fibre
51g carb ♥ 0.6g salt

160